The Spiritual Needs of Children

A Guide for Nurses, Parents and Teachers

Judith Allen Shelly and Others

InterVarsity Press
Downers Grove
Illinois 60515

InterVarsity Press is the book-publishing division of Inter-Varsity Christian Fellowship, a student movement active on campus at hundreds of universities, colleges and schools of nursing. For information about local and regional activities, write IVCF, 233 Langdon St., Madison, WI 53703.

Distributed in Canada through InterVarsity Press, 1875 Leslie St., Unit 10, Don Mills, Ontario M3B 2M5, Canada.

Scripture quotations, unless otherwise stated, are from the Revised Standard Version of the Bible, copyrighted 1946, 1952, © 1971, 1973. Verses marked TLB are taken from The Living Bible, copyright 1971 by Tyndale House Publishers, Wheaton, Ill. Used by permission.

ISBN 0-87784-381-3

Printed in the United States of America

Library of Congress Cataloging in Publication Data

Shelly, Judith Allen.
    The spiritual needs of children.

    Includes bibliographical references.
    1. Children—Religious life.   2. Sick children—
Religious life.   I. Title.
BV4571.2.S47   248.8'6   82-7223
ISBN 0-87784-381-3   AACR2

| 17 | 16 | 15 | 14 | 13 | 12 | 11 | 10 | 9 | 8 | 7 | 6 | 5 | 4 | 3 | 2 | 1 |
| 95 | 94 | 93 | 92 | 91 | 90 | 89 | 88 | 87 | 86 | 85 | 84 | 83 | 82 | | | |

Foreword

Recently I renewed acquaintance with a nursing colleague. When I told her I had been asked to write the foreword to a book on the spiritual needs of children, she responded, "Great! We have been assessing every other need of children; it's about time we paid attention to that one."

I would not call my friend religious, but she does recognize a neglected dimension of care. This concern is felt by nurses, physicians, chaplains, social workers and others who work in hospitals with children and parents:

■ the staff nurse on the evening shift who is embarrassed when a little girl facing surgery tomorrow asks if she will listen to her prayers

■ the nursing student who is told by a school-age boy that he does not think he will mind dying since his mother said he would see God

■ the parent whose child asks again and again, "Why am I sick? Does God hate me?"

■ the Sunday-school teacher who tries to comfort the crying boy who does not want to go to heaven if he has to leave his dog behind

■ the social worker who must arrange care for a widower whose school-age daughter is dying

■ the medical student confronted by the father of a deformed newborn; the father cries out his hatred of a God who would allow such things to happen

■ the primary nurse who is asked by a family member for help in finding some comforting Bible verses

■ the hospital chaplain who has counseled adult patients who fear anesthesia and possible death but has not talked to children in the same situation

■ the intensive care unit nurse who longs for the right words to comfort a suffering child—she knows that not all suffering is physical and relieved by medication

The concept of whole-person health care is a relatively recent development. For years the medical professions assumed that hospitals run by religious groups would give some attention to spiritual needs. In secular hospitals, on the other hand, the patient's religion was a private matter and could be dealt with by calling in the patient's own priest, pastor or rabbi. In children's hospitals, spiritual needs were usually left to parents. For years, fears of death and dying were hushed up as inappropriate for conversation, or like sex, were met with "Ask your mother or father when they come in."

True, there are nurses who hear the nighttime prayers of youngsters and who read from a child's favorite Bible storybooks. There are also instances in which hospital staff members conduct small Sunday-school classes for children. Only recently, however, have children's hospitals employed chaplains or made any effort to provide more than a chapel for private meditation and prayer. Chaplains, as well as other hospital personnel, find it very difficult to deal with the complex situations and crises presented by children and families who populate children's hospitals.

Shortly after the publication of *Spiritual Care: The Nurse's Role,* the Eastern Regional Advisory and Work Committee (ERAWC) of Nurses Christian Fellowship discussed the possibility of establishing a task force on the spiritual needs of children. The task force would consist of professionals representing several areas of child care including social work, nursing, medicine, education and chaplaincy, as well as parents. An ad hoc committee of the ERAWC was charged with exploring the idea; I was privileged to chair that committee. After months of work the task force met October 19-20, 1979 at the Children's Hospital of Philadelphia. The results of those brainstorming sessions have been one workshop which took place in March 1980—and this book.

To the task force on the spiritual needs of children I would like to express a special word of gratitude. Without their hard work and wise counsel this book could never have been written.

Joseph Bayly, B.A., Th.M.; theologian and parent; Bartlett, Illinois

Mary Lou Bayly, B.A.; Christian educator and parent; Bartlett, Illinois

Hope Brooks, M.D.; pediatric oncologist; Philadelphia

Mae Shirley Cook; Handi*Vangelism Fellowship; Philadelphia

Robert Ekeland, A.C.S.W.; associate professor of social work; St. Davids, Pennsylvania

Janet K. Hesse, M.S.N.; nursing instructor; Chester, Pennsylvania

Lois J. Hopkins, M.S.N.Ed.; associate professor of nursing; Kent, Ohio

June Lynn Jones, M.S.N.; assistant professor of nursing; Cincinnati, Ohio

H. Elaine McCaully, M.S.N.; nursing instructor; Villanova,

Pennsylvania

Susan K. Reed, B.S.N.; pediatric staff nurse; Norfolk, Virginia

Jane Corwin Reeves, B.S.N.; parent; Biloxi, Mississippi

Barbara Prins Ritsema, M.S.N.; nursing supervisor; Philadelphia

Jack L. Rodgers, M. Div.; pediatric hospital chaplain; Philadelphia

Janet V. Snyder, M.Ed.; nursery school teacher; Philadelphia

Susan Stanhope, B.S.N.; staff nurse; Patterson, New York

Dianne Stannard, B.S.N.; staff nurse; Chicago

Marcia Thompson, M.A.R.; Christian educator; Berlin, West Germany

Judith Van Heukelem, M.S.N.; NCF regional director; Belmont, California

Melanie English Van Sant, M.S.N.; nursing instructor; Newark, Delaware

Michele Vicari, R.N.; staff nurse; Chicago

Cynthia Wood, B.S.N.; staff nurse; Minnetonka, Minnesota

Erna I. Goulding, R.N., M.A.
Associate Vice President for Patient Care
Children's Hospital of Philadelphia

Chapter One
Jesus & the Children: A Mandate to Care
Judith Allen Shelly

Last night a tiny voice said over the phone, "Jesus died on the cross for my sins. They put nails in his hands and he died... but on Easter he came alive!" My three-and-a-half-year-old nephew, Allen, continued on the subject for a while, then switched to chocolate Easter bunnies.

"Does he know what he's talking about?" I asked my sister.

"I'm not sure, but he has been talking about death all week, ever since he heard in nursery school about Jesus' dying on the cross," she replied.

How much do children understand about religious concepts? Most experts in child development argue that children understand very little about abstract religious concepts before age twelve, yet

Allen certainly had his facts straight and was applying them to his life.

"Let the Children Come"

Are children capable of a meaningful relationship with God? Stories abound of very young children who made serious and lasting commitments to God. A missionary leaving for the field reports that she committed her life to Christ as a five-year-old because of the influence of a nurse while she was in the hospital. A physician tells that at age eight, he promised God that he would become a doctor after he watched helplessly while his younger brother died of a mysterious illness. A young woman recalls how exciting it was to hear in Sunday school that she was a "daughter of the King" because she was one of God's children. Her self-image was deeply enhanced because from then on she thought of herself as a princess.

Wayne Oates, professor of psychology of religion at Southern Baptist Theological Seminary, writes, "One of the greatest truths that come to us through the developmental study of personality is that religion is communicated differently at different stages of development of a person. . . . The whole religious quest consists of opening the doors of childhood to the incursions of the Eternal."[1]

Jesus put it more simply, "Let the children come to me, and do not hinder them; for to such belongs the kingdom of heaven" (Mt 19:14). Children have always been attracted to Jesus, and he never told them they had to wait until they fully understood all the theological concepts before they could come to him. He did not preach to them or reprimand them; instead, he "laid his hands on them" (19:15)—he touched them—and exhorted adults to "turn and become like children" (18:3).

Children hold a special place in the heart of God. Calling a child to him, Jesus told his disciples, "Whoever humbles himself like this child, he is the greatest in the kingdom of heaven" (18:4). Think about that. How humble would you feel if Jesus called you over and told everyone around you that you were the greatest?

What a boost to the child's self-concept! Obviously, the humility Jesus commended did not rule out a positive self-regard and a need for affirmation and encouragement.

The word used in Matthew 18 for *humble* connotes dependence and submission to authority, not self-abasement. A little girl may think she is the center of the universe, but she knows she is dependent on her parents. To a great extent, parents represent God to any young child, but God is not limited by this arrangement. He often breaks through to communicate directly with a child, especially with one who is seriously ill. Children seem to sense the mysterious presence of God and know their dependence on him.

The characteristic of children which makes them the greatest in the kingdom of heaven also makes them tremendously vulnerable in the kingdom of this world. The American Nurses Association's "Report on the Hearings on the Unmet Needs of Children and Youth" (1979) reveals major areas where the dependency and vulnerability of children leave them open to difficulties such as drug abuse, child abuse and sexual exploitation.[2] Jesus recognized the potential for trouble and exhorted his disciples, "Whoever receives one such child in my name receives me; but whoever causes one of these little ones who believe in me to sin, it would be better for him to have a great millstone fastened round his neck and to be drowned in the depth of the sea" (Mt 18:5-6). Adult caretakers are given awesome responsibilities for the nurture of God's children: first, a positive command to receive them in his name; second, a negative warning to guard against causing them to sin.

Receiving a child in the name of Jesus simply means loving him or her as Jesus does. That love is so consistent that children feel safe and secure, assured that their needs will be met (1 Jn 4:18). It is a love so unconditional that they do not have to repress their real selves in order to please; they know they are accepted as they are (Rom 3:23-25). It is a love which seeks the very best for the child and is sometimes expressed as firm discipline (Heb 12:6). It is a warm, touching love, which is personal and treats each individual as special (Mt 18:12-14; 19:15). Finally, it is a love which recognizes its Source, and does not seek personal gain and glory (Is 43:1-7). Oates states, "God encounters a person through other redemptive personalities or communities around the individual."³ Ideally, the first "redemptive personalities" are the parents, then expand to include the rest of the family, the church, the neighborhood, the school and the health care community.

Looking after Lambs

Jesus' warning against causing a child to sin is a bit unsettling. It may seem to imply the obvious evils of drug dealing and sexual abuse, but adults cause children to sin in many subtle ways which may not appear so villainous on the surface. Sin is anything which causes a person to turn away from God. Adults represent God to children by everything they say and do. If adults communicate to children that they do not care, cannot be trusted, have unrealistic expectations or intend to hurt them, children may transfer these attributes to God. Some such children never develop a healthy relationship with God.

Jesus became indignant when his disciples prevented children from coming to him (Mk 10:14). The disciples probably felt that their Lord had more important things to do and did not want him to be bothered. How many times do we keep children away from Jesus? How many times do we become so caught up in the "more important things" of medicines, treatments and hospital routines that we neglect to ask a hospitalized child if he or she usually prays before eating or sleeping, or if Bible stories are part of the daily routine?

Each child is so precious to God that Jesus compared his concern to that of a man who had a flock of one hundred sheep. One of them got lost, so the man left the rest of the flock and searched everywhere until he found the one who went astray (Mt 18:10-14). He expects no less of those who care for his lambs—parents, teachers, nurses and other significant adults.

This book is concerned primarily with the spiritual care of children. Because the spiritual infuses and enlivens the whole person, however, physical, emotional and social needs will often be intertwined in the chapters which follow. A spiritual need is "the lack of any factor or factors necessary to establish and/or maintain a dynamic, personal relationship with God."[4] More simply put, it is any need which, if not met, hinders a child from coming to Jesus.

The basic spiritual needs of adults outlined in *Spiritual Care: The Nurse's Role* also hold true for children. The need for *meaning and purpose* develops into more sophisticated forms as the child matures, but it is present from infancy.[5] The need for *love and relatedness* is basic to survival. Babies who are unloved become seriously emotionally disturbed, or may even die. As the growing child becomes secure in the love of parents and other caring adults, he or she begins to love others and understand God's love. The need for *forgiveness* first shows itself as the need for unqualified love, then gradually develops into a need to be redeemed from "naughtiness."

The childhood years, especially the first twelve years, are crucial to spiritual development. Proverbs 22:6 states, "Train up a child in the way he should go, and when he is old he will not depart from it." The ancient wisdom of the Scriptures is validated by psychological research: the spiritual understanding developed by a child in the first twelve years may be temporarily questioned in adolescence, but it will usually form the basis for religious beliefs in adulthood.[6] The beliefs of most adults are very similar to their parents' beliefs.

The primary burden of responsibility for the spiritual care of children falls on parents. Good nursing care sees the child as part of a family network, not as an isolated patient. Spiritual care is no exception. Parents must be supported and respected when spiritual care is offered. In times of crisis, nurses, teachers, pastors and others who are willing to spiritually support and encourage parents and their children will have a lasting impact. Each childhood crisis has the potential to be a spiritual crisis. When their child suffers innocently parents frequently ask, "Why? What did

I do to cause this? Is God punishing me?" The child's healthy spiritual development is also tremendously disrupted. Physical pain and the feeling of abandonment while in a hospital, surrounded by frightening equipment, threaten the child's fragile development of trust and sense of self-worth. Spiritual care is not merely a nice option for nurses who have a few spare moments; it is essential for the child's total development and outlook on life. We have a mandate to care, not only as faithful Christians, but also as responsible care-givers.

Part I
Spiritual
Growth &
Development

To care well for children, nurses must learn how they grow and develop physically, emotionally, mentally and socially. The needs and abilities of children differ according to stages of development. The nurse who gives a detailed, logical explanation of a medical procedure to a two-year-old quickly discovers that it is as futile as telling a fifteen-year-old that he must do what he is told without questioning. Although the importance of developmental theories is assumed in physical care and patient teaching, we sometimes fail to apply it to spiritual care. We often expect the young child to understand abstract theological concepts and demand that the teen-ager accept puzzling perplexities "on faith" without asking questions.

One question arises immediately: Can there be growth before there is birth? If not, how can we determine when spiritual birth takes place? Some theological traditions assume that spiritual birth occurs at baptism in infancy. Others insist that spiritual birth occurs with a "born again" experience of accepting Jesus Christ as Lord and Savior. Neither tradition, however, would deny that God works in children before they are baptized or make a formal profession of faith. Just as there is physical growth and development before physical birth, there is spiritual growth and development before spiritual birth. Proper care and nourishment will facilitate the birth—of either type—of a healthy child.

Spiritual development is interrelated with physical and psychosocial development. Developmental psychologists do not agree about the stages of development or even if definable stages exist, but their observations about the way children think provide clues to how children respond to religious teaching and spiritual intervention. An understanding of developmental tasks can alert us to appropriate times to challenge and encourage children in their spiritual development.

Many cognitive psychologists do not subscribe to a stage theory. They assert that the important element is not age level but the experiences that usually occur at these levels.[1] Havighurst and Keating state: "One form of appropriate experience is direct experience of the presence of God. Clearly, children who have such experiences are equipped differently for their development of religious beliefs than children who do not have a direct personal experience of a mystical nature."[2] When children are constantly nourished in the faith through prayer and Bible teaching in the context of a loving family and supportive Christian community, they are likely to encounter the living God and develop a deep and stable faith. Occasionally, a nurse will encounter a very sick child who has had little or no instruction in the Christian faith but who knows God and has an unshakeable faith. We cannot limit God to working in the proper ages and stages, or through the "right" channels, but we can observe that he usually does.

Research in spiritual development is limited and often conflicting. Large samplings in secular settings are difficult to obtain, so most studies have been conducted among children in churches, Christian schools and other Christian settings. Most studies were not well controlled and do not measure important variables. Many researchers lack a hypothetical framework, thus reducing the value of the findings. Others have been so bound by a particular age-stage theory that they fail to consider important factors such as the family setting, church affiliation, differences in religious outlook between the parents and the way members of a particular church relate to the surrounding community. Piaget's developmental theories have dominated the research on religious development, although other important researchers have differed in their findings.[3]

The following chapters take an eclectic approach to spiritual development with an attempt to put it in the context of one-to-one relationships between parents and their children, and the nurse and the child. Summaries of how various aspects of spiritual development fit into the theories of Erikson and Piaget are provided (see Tables 1 and 2) because these theories are usually taught in schools of nursing. Each provides a different emphasis and complements the other. Neither is the final authority. The study of spiritual development is a wide-open field with a great need for solid research from a nursing perspective.

Table 1
Piaget's Stages of Cognitive Development As Related to Spiritual Development

Sensorimotor Stage (under age 2)—Understanding of God is vague, associated with parents. Prayer may provide comfort and deepen bond between parents, child and God. Responds to environment of love and warmth. No sense of conscience. Wise use of diversion better than punishment for wrongdoing.

Preoperational Stage (about ages 2-7)—Anthropomorphic view of God, physical characteristics predominate. Beginning to understand God as Creator. Meaning of prayer vague, but prayer rituals become important. Understands simple Bible stories with one clear theme. Visual aids reinforce words and ideas, especially if they can be touched and manipulated. Conscience beginning to emerge. Young preschooler behaves for fear of punishment; later behavior is based on a desire to please. Sees right and wrong as absolutes. Can be taught to love Jesus and want to please him. Major area of spiritual growth is in forming attitudes toward God, the Bible and the church.

Concrete Operational Stage (about ages 7-12)—God described according to his actions (he loves, helps, watches over us). Growing sense of personal relationship with God. Prayer consists of making verbal requests to God, gradually developing into a private conversation with God as the child matures. Understands cause and effect relationships, scientific facts, mathematical computation and reasoning. Bible understanding is concrete and fact-oriented, but can begin to apply it to daily life. Conscience continues to develop, begins to see moral decisions in their context. Commitment based more on a desire to please Jesus than from a deep sense of sin. Sin viewed as specific acts of misbehavior rather than rebellion against God.

Formal Abstract Operational Stage (over age 12)—Sees God as personal friend and confidant. Focuses on attributes such as mercy, omnipresence, omnipotence and omniscience. Prayer remains a private conversation with God, but greater emphasis on thanksgiving and sharing intimacies, less on personal requests. Able to deal with meaning of biblical material beyond facts, and sees how it fits into God's overall plan. Abstract reasoning facilitates understanding of symbolic literature, empathy, introspection, idealism and philosophizing. Establishing own value system based on internal rationale. Concerned about meaning and purpose in life. The problem of evil in the world and the significance of God's grace become meaningful.

References
Eleanor Daniel, John W. Wade and Charles Gresham, *Introduction to Christian Education* (Cincinnati: Standard Publishing, 1980).
David Elkind, "The Development of Religious Understanding in Children and Adolescents," Merton P. Strommen, ed., *Research on Religious Development* (New York: Hawthorn Books, 1971), pp. 655-85.
Susie M. Setzer, "The Adolescent Thinker," *Learning With,* February 1981, pp. 3-5.

Table 2
Outline of Spiritual Development As Related to Erikson's Eight Ages of Man*
Lois J. Hopkins, M.S.N.

Prenatal Period—Developing child's environment is influenced by love, joy, good health. Preparation of parents for task of child-rearing includes their own spiritual well-being, as well as plans for the child's religious upbringing.

Birth to Age One—Stage of basic trust vs. basic mistrust. Child needs a dependable environment, security in care, and love from a mother figure. Ability to trust, which develops during this stage, is essential for a growing faith in God.

Age One to Three—Stage of autonomy vs. shame and doubt. Child needs love balanced with consistent discipline (e.g., wise use of distraction). Healthy self-concept lays a foundation for growing ability to be intimate with others and with God.

Age Three to Six—Stage of initiative vs. guilt. Needs to know unconditional love from other people and from God. Unrealistic demands for child's behavior at this stage may cause child to later reject God or to become legalistic in religious practices. Parent's religious observances of Christmas, Easter, grace at meals and daily devotions greatly influence the child at this stage.

Age Six to Twelve—Stage of industry vs. inferiority. Conscience is developing. Rules are important in both games and religious observances. Begins to question parents' authority and knowledge as the influence of teachers and peers is felt more and more. Can now distinguish between God and parents (or other adults). Growing understanding of sin and forgiveness.

Age Twelve to Eighteen—Stage of identity vs. role confusion. Adolescent rebellion against parents may include rejection of the religious beliefs of their upbringing. Becomes more interested in a personal relationship with God, but may be opposed to institutional religion. Often begins asking deep religious questions, but hesitates to discuss them with peers for fear of ridicule.

---

*Erik H. Erikson, *Childhood and Society,* 2nd ed. (New York: W. W. Norton & Co., 1963), pp. 247-63.

Chapter Two
Foundations for Faith: The First Five Years
Judith Allen Shelly & Others

The spiritual development of a child begins at conception, initiated by the Holy Spirit. From the very beginning God not only shapes our physical bodies but also instills in our lives meaning and purpose. The psalmist proclaims:

For thou didst form my inward parts,
> thou didst knit me together in my mother's womb. . . .

Thou knowest me right well;
> my frame was not hidden from thee,

This chapter is edited by Judith Allen Shelly and is based on contributions by Lois J. Hopkins, June Lynn Jones, Janet V. Snyder, Susan F. Stanhope, Donna D. Stewart and Melanie E. Van Sant.

when I was being made in secret,
    intricately wrought in the depths of the earth.
Thy eyes beheld my unformed substance;
    in thy book were written, every one of them,
the days that were formed for me,
    when as yet there was none of them. (Ps 139:13-16)
Foundations for faith are laid not only in the child himself, but also
in the parents as they grow in their own relationships to God and
to one another. Spirituality develops as the child responds to God
at work in his or her life.[1] Parents and other caretakers prepare
the infant for spiritual development by providing a loving, trust-
worthy environment which draws strength and stability from their
own faith.

Trust: The First Step
The first developmental task of the infant, according to Erikson,
is to develop basic trust.[2] Trust is essential not only for self-control
and human relationships but also for faith, through which the
growing child relates to God. The quality of the mother-child relationship is the most important factor in nurturing the development of basic trust. Even at the earliest stages of growth infants
benefit from their parents' intrinsic faith and religious commitment. Erikson states:

> The parental faith which supports the trust emerging in the new-
> born, has throughout history sought its institutional safeguard
> . . . in organized religion. Trust born of care is, in fact, the touch-
> stone of the *actuality* of a given religion. . . . The clinician can
> only observe that many are proud to be without religion whose
> children cannot afford their being without it.[3]

Psychiatrist Paul D. Meier notes that "psychological development
will enable our children to live in society and to earn a living, but
spiritual development will enable them to understand the meaning of life."[4] The need for meaning is evident even in infancy.
Erikson asserts that parents must communicate a sense of meaning in the way they guide their children because "ultimately, chil-

dren become neurotic not from frustrations, but from the lack or loss of societal meaning in these frustrations."[5] Because the spiritual stability of the parents is so essential to the spiritual development of their children, we cannot consider one without the other.

The neonatal intensive care unit is an environment in which spiritual needs are obvious but rarely met.[6] After months of preparation and anticipation for the birth of a child, life suddenly becomes a series of hour-to-hour clinical reports and respirator settings, invasion of veins and arteries by plastic cannulas, and scans and monitors surrounding the infant so joyfully awaited. A team of strangers close around a baby who was intended to be nurtured and sheltered in the loving privacy of the family. Nurses' attempts (or failures) to help parents assimilate the meaning of these circumstances may greatly influence the spiritual development of the child.

Newborn infants respond primarily to satisfaction of biological needs such as hunger, but they may not survive without a dependable, loving, nurturing mother figure. Both parents should be encouraged to hold and caress their baby, even with all the tubes and wires attached. Parents can be urged to establish eye contact with their child, to sing to and pray for him or her. The nurse may have to serve in this role if the mother is absent, but our primary focus must be to promote the parent-infant bond. Strengthening the mother's and father's parenting skills increases their basic security, and subsequently the security of the baby. The illness of an infant may intensify parents' anxieties and fears. They often feel helpless and unable to communicate their love and concern to their child. Parents may also feel overwhelmingly guilty over their child's illness. They may blame themselves for causing the illness by things they did, or failed to do, during pregnancy. Some parents feel that their child's illness is punishment from God for their sins.

In time, physical and emotional needs become intertwined, and the baby begins to recognize his or her parents and becomes anxious when separated from them. Memory is sufficiently developed between five and nine months to remember frequent injections or frightening treatments. As soon as a painful procedure is completed the baby needs to be comforted and shown that the associated equipment is put away. Memory and behavior are healthy ego responses which anticipate danger and afford protection. If a child is not forewarned and shown the equipment before the procedure begins, he or she cannot marshall defenses in preparation. Such infants will consider the nurse and their worlds untrustworthy and fearful, laying a shaky foundation for later spiritual growth.

Toddling toward Autonomy

As the infant becomes a toddler autonomy becomes the major developmental task.[7] It is also the peak age for separation anxiety. Great harm can be done if toddlers are separated from their parents for a long time. They need frequent daily contact with their parents. In the case of hospitalized toddlers, if rooming-in is not feasible, parents should be encouraged to visit as often as possible and maintain contact through phone calls, having family pictures in clear view, and leaving tape recordings of family members. Parents should be encouraged to be truthful about when they will return.

The conflict between the toddler's increasing move toward autonomy and fear of separation from parents is a crucial developmental phase in spiritual development. Consider Tommy, for example. If he learns that his parents will not allow him to be himself (within the limits of safety), he may outwardly conform to their expectations in order to gain approval but inwardly resent their authority and question his own self-worth. Later he may resent God. If as a toddler he is given too much freedom, he may come to the frightening conclusion that he is in charge of his world and develop a protective shell of toughness. When Tommy discovers that his parents are unreliable protectors and disciplinarians, he may later question God's reliability—or even his existence.

A toddler who is nurtured in an atmosphere that balances love with consistent discipline should develop a healthy self-concept. This lays the groundwork for a growing ability to be intimate with others and with God. During the preschool years a child may easily be overcome by a multitude of natural affronts to personal self-worth during the "initiative versus guilt" stage defined by Erikson.[8] The child is small and powerless in a world where most decisions are made by adults. Lack of coordination, experience and knowledge further reduce a child's sense of self-worth. Additional problems such as illness, handicaps and separation from parents may further wound the self-concept, fostering feelings of guilt, inferiority and inadequacy.

The interpersonal relationships among adults who care for a child, at home or in the health care setting, are important spiritual influences. Genuine love and fellowship, and mutual respect among professionals are essential for healthy psychological and spiritual development in children. Religious beliefs and customs, when practiced regularly in an atmosphere of love, are also extremely important to toddlers and preschoolers. Mealtime grace, bedtime prayers and Bible stories, and going to Sunday school and church can be deeply meaningful and comforting.

The Comfort of the Routine

Two-year-old Amy stood in her crib shrieking, "Pay! Pay!" while her bewildered babysitter sought the cause of her distress. She reviewed the bedtime routine—brushing teeth, potty, pajamas, a drink, a Bible story, a good-night kiss, Raggedy Ann, a favorite blanket, tucking her in, turning off the light, leaving the door ajar. She did not think she had missed anything, but Amy continued to cry out, "Pay! Pay!" Suddenly she realized that Amy was trying to say, "Pray!" She went back in, sat down and prayed with Amy, who then contentedly snuggled up to Raggedy Ann and went to sleep.

Routines such as prayer before meals and at bedtime should be continued in the hospital. Familiar pictures of Jesus and other Bible characters can also comfort children. Three-year-old Susan was tearful and apprehensive when admitted to the hospital, but then in the playroom she saw a large picture of Jesus and the children. She looked up with surprise and delight and said, "Oh! It's Jesus!" She settled down and began playing with the toys.

Parents are chiefly responsible for a child's spiritual development and basic self-concept. Nurses share this responsibility when they serve as parent substitutes during hospitalization, as role models in interpersonal relationships and as supportive, caring adults. Concepts of the world develop for a preschooler through sensory experiences. In other words, what a preschooler learns about the world must be experienced. The nature of God is demonstrated to children in this age group through interactions with warm, sensitive, caring Christian adults. When asked to draw a picture of God, one four-year-old drew a human form surrounded by a colorful assortment of circles, squares and triangles (see Figure 1). She explained, "It's a person and my mommy giving me a kiss. My mommy loves God." The experiences of limit setting and discipline may also affect a child's view of God. Another child drew God as a large figure hovering over three rather cheerful figures and explained, "God is going to get mad because no one is good" (see Figure 2).

Preschool children expect immediate punishment for misbehavior. Illness, death of a family member, altered diets, painful treatments and injuries are often viewed as deprivation and punishment. The problem is exacerbated when parents have used "going to the doctor," "shots" or other medical treatments as threatened punishment. A child may feel that God is demanding punishment for some remembered or imagined wrong. By the end of the preschool stage, many children are sensitive to wrongdoing and are concerned that God sees what they do. Caring adults must constantly reinforce that God loves them just the way they are. He does not make children sick because they misbehave.

"Mommy, There's God!"

Guidelines for the preschooler's behavior should be set according to what is realistic for the developmental stage. A rigid code of unrealistic conduct, whether in the home or in the hospital, will build a sense of failure and false guilt. Adults are the earliest reflection of God to a child. Meier notes that children from homes which expect unattainable behavior will eventually either reject God as nonexistent, or will see him as a stern, distant God who exists but whom they must constantly try to placate through works.[9]

Preschool children are concrete in their thinking. They tend to think of God in literal terms and cannot separate him from parents and other authority figures. In drawings by preschoolers God wears pants and a shirt. He has hands, feet, cheeks, a beard, a wife . . . and eats with a fork (see Figures 3-10). Many a young child has pointed to the minister in church and said, "Mommy, there's God!" Children may also point to pictures in a Bible storybook and ask, "Is this God?" Some confusion can be avoided by focusing on Jesus because they can readily identify with his birth as a baby and life as a human being. Preschool children love Bible stories, especially those with plenty of action. They can begin to understand that God loves them and that he created them. In their egocentric view of the world, though, they may not give God exclusive rights to creation. Four-year-old George explained his drawing of a large purple mass next to a small squiggle by saying, "I am making God's bones. He's building a building" (Figure 11).

Children need adult caretakers who are dependable and consistent to foster the continued development of trust. When adults are inconsistent and unreliable a child learns not to rely on the environment or God. Unfortunately many situations in health care settings undermine a child's trust in parents, the nurse and other members of the health care team. Promises are made which cannot be kept ("No more shots" or "This won't hurt" or "I'll be right here"). Unscheduled delays and interruptions, a change in doctor's orders, or unexpected complications make the staff appear inconsistent. Unavoidable conflicts which delay parents' visits, as well as worries and responsibilities at home, may make parents seem preoccupied and undependable. A child may become fearful and insecure. Explaining why the event happened and saying you are sorry may help to restore trust.

Children are quick to recognize when they are not being told the truth. Dishonesty about coming events ("You will feel wonderful after you have your tonsils out, and you can have all the ice cream you want") or outright lies (telling a terminally ill child, "You'll be just fine and be able to run and play real soon") can seriously affect a child's developing sense of trust. Many parents slip out quietly while a child is sleeping to avoid a tearful parting. The child awakens feeling betrayed and abandoned. He or she needs to be told honestly what is happening, even if it is painful.

The subject of death often fascinates young children. Some casually say, "Yesterday I was dead," meaning "I was sick" or simply "I was not in school." Death is usually associated with separation or departure which, though distressing, is temporary. It may be seen as punishment for wrongdoing, or as a way of removing frustrations. A child may say to her mother, "I wish you were dead!" meaning that she is angry because her mother is preventing her from having her own way. She has no concept of death as a permanent separation.

Death and God are often related in a child's thinking. In a class of twenty-six four- and five-year-olds who were asked to draw a picture of God, three (twelve per cent) drew things associated with death. In one, God is taking a dead baby up to the sky, which could be a convenient way to get rid of an attention-getting new sibling (Figure 12). In another a mommy takes a dead baby to the hospital and "God makes her come home safely" (Figure 13). It is not known whether this was fantasy, or if it depicted a sick baby who went to the hospital and recovered (or a mother who went to the hospital to give birth). The third child drew herself as dead and lying on a bed with a smile on her face, with a smiling God beside her. She says, "This is God and he's taking me up to the sky because I died and that's the blood" (Figure 14).

Understanding What Death Is

A child's understanding of death is influenced by his experiences. A child who has seen an animal struck by a car on the road or has seen seriously ill or deformed children in the hospital may view death as mutilation. Those who have lost a close relative may see it as abandonment. Death may also be associated with immobility such as traction, restraints or nonmovement. Although they may be unable to verbalize their fears, they may be able to work them out by drawing or by playing with dolls or puppets.[10]

Children as young as three know when they have a fatal illness or are near death. Separation from parents by death becomes a growing realization for young children even when no one tells them. Spiritual development is often accelerated in dying children, who may display a wisdom beyond their years. Sarah was dying of leukemia. Tears flowed from her mother's eyes as she cradled the toddler in her arms. Sarah reached up and patted her mother on the cheek, saying, "It's okay, Mommy. God will take care of me." Three-year-old Tina, in the terminal stage of cystic fibrosis, seemed especially anxious when she was readmitted to the hospital after a brief time at home. Her mother tried to reassure her that she would be coming home again soon, but Tina responded, "No, tonight I'm going to heaven with Jesus." She died that evening.

Preschoolers begin to learn basic concepts about God and to trust him. Psychiatrist Philip Barker asserts: "While very broad emotional attitudes to the world have become established in the first two years, these are filled in and elaborated during the subsequent years. If religious beliefs are to be acquired, the appropriate attitudes should be learnt from the parents at this time."[11]

What children do not learn from their parents they will pick up from friends, baby sitters and other significant adults. Jenny, age four, told her grandmother in vivid detail about the Sunday-school class she claimed she attended. She told about the songs she sang, the pictures she colored, and the Bible lesson studied. Her grandmother was delighted and told Jenny's mother that she was pleased that they were taking Jenny to Sunday school again. The mother replied, "Jenny just made that up. She hasn't been to Sunday school in six months!"

Sunday school and church can be extremely significant to preschoolers. They enjoy going (unless they have had bad experiences) and often prod their parents into attending church. Preschoolers will also insist that parents practice religious customs learned in school or in the homes of other children. Five-year-old Michelle learned to hold hands around the dinner table and thank God for the food while visiting a friend. When she came home she insisted on instituting the same practice with her own family.

Dorothy Marlow asserts that a child cannot be kept spiritually neutral.[12] Children have a natural interest in God and an inborn sense of the divine, the numinous, which must be nurtured by the family and community. Parents and other adult caretakers will help to determine if future spiritual growth and development will be healthy or unhealthy by their actions and attitudes during these formative years. Three basic ingredients lay a healthy foundation for spiritual development: unconditional love with plenty of positive reinforcement, realistic discipline which holds children responsible for their actions within the limits of their abilities, and a support system which is dependable and truthful.

Figure 1/"It's a person and my mommy giving me a kiss. My mommy loves God." Susan

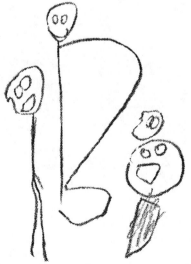

Figure 2/"God is going to get mad because no one is good." Paula

Figure 3/"This is God in his pants. He has some cheeks and a beard." Fred

Figure 4/"God is wearing a striped shirt and he is waving to someone." Melanie

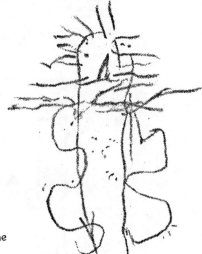

Figure 5/"This is God. First I made some arms and then legs and a moustache and feet, knees and a hat.
He has a shirt on. He loves people." Roger

Figure 6/"This is God. He has legs, eyes, nose, mouth, hair and some hands." Richard

Figure 7/"God's feet."   Robin

Figure 8/"This is God's wife."   Jessica

Figure 9/"This is God picking up a fork to eat his dinner."   Jenny

Figure 10/"This is God looking at somebody."   Adam

Figure 12/"This is the baby that is dead. God takes the baby up in the sky." Becky

Figure 11/"I am making God's bones. He's building a building." George

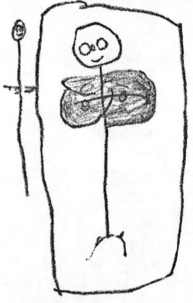

Figure 13/"It's a house with a baby. The ..iommy is watching the baby and the baby is dead. Her mom takes her to the hospital and God makes her come home safely." Elizabeth

Figure 14/"This is God and he's taking me to the sky because I died and that's the blood." Lynn

Chapter Three
Growing in Grace: The School-age Child
Judith Allen Shelly & Others

How do you know that Jesus is your friend?" I asked children in each Sunday-school class one morning.

Four-year-old Tracy replied, "He loves me."

"How do you know that?" I asked.

"I don't know . . . he just does," she answered.

Six-year-old Bobby was more explicit, "He takes care of my cat."

Eight-year-old Melissa told me she knows Jesus is her friend

This chapter is edited by Judith Allen Shelly and is based on contributions by Lois J. Hopkins, Janet V. Snyder, Marcia Thompson and Melanie Van Sant.

because, "I can talk to him."

Ten-year-old Marti answered with an air of·authority, "I know because he died on the cross for my sins." Asked to explain what that means, she replied, "It means he loves me, even if I'm bad."

Twelve-year-old Roger looked puzzled, then replied, "Sometimes I'm not so sure he is my friend."

A Time to Grow 5 ~ 8

Psychoanalysts refer to the elementary school years as the "latency period" because psychosexual development is at a lull, but the term is deceptive. It is a time of rapid physical, intellectual, social and spiritual growth. Erikson calls the years between six and twelve the age of "industry vs. inferiority," a time when children learn to win recognition by producing things.[1] In school they learn the basic skills—both academic and social—for succeeding in society. Spiritually, they become acquainted with the basic content of their faith. Conscience begins to mature. Understanding of sin and forgiveness grows. Rules become important in religious observance, as well as in games. A child can now distinguish between God and parents (or other adults). They may also make a distinction between God the Father and Jesus. They also begin to question parents' authority and knowledge as the influence of teachers is felt more and more. The peer group becomes increasingly important; it is painful to be different.

Thinking is still concrete, but a school-age child begins to use abstract concepts to describe God. Marlow postulates that "probably his greatest achievement in abstract thought is his beginning interest in the concept of a power greater than himself or his parents—God."[2]

Children at this age have a great desire to learn about God and heaven. They like to recite standard prayers at bedtime and mealtime. Some think that animals can pray, too, and expect their pets to "fold their paws" when they pray. They enjoy Bible stories, though their ability to think about concepts and figure out analogies is limited. Biblical parables which require applying principles to everyday life are difficult. For instance, Tommy, age seven, was asked to draw his favorite Bible story (Figure 15). Asked to explain the drawing, he said: "This is the story of the good Americans. This guy here got mugged—he's all bloody. This guy here [walking on next hill] is the minister. He had to get to church, so he couldn't stop and help him. This guy here [in green at far right] is in the choir. He had to get to church too. These guys [in helicopters, in jet and on ground, saying, "OK"] are the good Americans. They came to help." (See Lk 10:29-37.) Asked what the story meant, Tommy explained that "the Americans are always the good guys." The fact that his father was an Army officer may have influenced the military manner in which the good Americans arrived.

Jean Piaget's observation that school-age children are unable to think abstractly leads some Christian educators to agree with Ronald Goldman that "it is an impossible task to teach the Bible as such to children much before adolescence."[3] If similar logic were applied to other subjects, the elementary school curriculum would be rather sparse. Other experts assert that the problem is not *whether* to teach the Bible, but *how* to teach it to children who think in concrete terms.[4] School-age children have an amazing ability to absorb information, which may become meaningful only after they are mature and have fully developed the ability to understand abstract concepts.

Most of this age group still picture God as a human figure. But unlike preschoolers who, when asked what God is like, describe him in physical terms, they tend to describe character traits or activities such as "God is everywhere. I love God and God loves me"; "God is love"; "God is happy. God makes flowers grow. God makes nice weather"; "God made the flowers and grass"; "God wishes everybody a happy Valentine's Day"; and "God helps us." (Figures 16-21, drawings by children of St. Luke's Lutheran Church School of Obelisk, Pa.) Jesus is usually identified as God (God has a brown or black beard in most of the drawings), the Son of God or a man, depending on their religious teaching.

As a child begins to realize that adults are fallible, he or she deeply needs assurance of someone or something greater. Adults who trust God and can communicate their faith without embarrassment will strengthen and comfort a child.[5]

School-age children think literally. Spiritual concepts take on materialistic and physical expression. Children accept metaphorical words at face value.[6] They believe in a literal God, a literal hell and a literal heaven. Heaven and hell fascinate them. The combination of a developing conscience and a concern about rules may cause a nagging sense of guilt and a fear of going to hell. Peter, age six, listened carefully to a Sunday-school lesson about Jesus' preparing a place for us in heaven, then raised his hand and asked, "But what if we don't get there?" He seemed satisfied with the teacher's explanation of the way that God provides for our salvation, and relieved at the reassurance he received.

Perception of guilt changes as a child matures. Piaget found that up to about age eight children judged degrees of guilt by the amount of damage done. Clumsiness was not differentiated from intentional destruction. For example, young schoolchildren did not consider the intent of children described in a series of stories about breakages. By age ten the children were able to consider the motivation of the culprits in the stories; thus, John, who innocently broke fifteen cups by opening a door, was not considered as guilty as Henry, who only broke one cup while trying to sneak some jam out of a cupboard.[7]

The tendency of younger children to associate clumsiness with guilt may influence their understanding of illness and hospitalization. They may view hospitalization as punishment for real or imagined wrong. A medical student who worked with children awaiting tonsillectomies asked them why their tonsils had to be removed.[8] They replied:

"I drank water too fast and got the hiccoughs."

"I sang too loud and hurt my throat."

"I went outside without my raincoat."

"I sucked my thumb. It must have messed them up."

Careful explanations by adults who will tell children that they did not cause their own illnesses may or may not be accepted, but should reduce anxiety. Children need to ask questions and talk about their illnesses. Those who have been told that "God sees all the bad things you do and he will punish you" may be afraid that he is punishing them by causing the illness. As they voice their fears and concerns, they can be reassured that God loves them and does not punish them by making them sick.

The Middle and Later Elementary Years

As children approach the middle elementary years (ages eight and nine) they exhibit not only a growing conscience but also an increasing understanding of forgiveness for wrongdoing. Eight-year-old Marci described God as "someone to talk to if you do something wrong."

Eight- and nine-year-olds begin to relate to God as individuals through spontaneous prayer. Their prayers are usually egocentric, asking God for personal favors, or thanking him for people and things they like. Although some magical expectation persists, they begin to recognize that God does not always do what they ask. Their increasing ability to reason usually leads them to rationalize that not everyone is served completely at once, so they do not become overly concerned about apparently unanswered prayers.

During the later elementary years (ages ten through twelve) children begin to judge their own and others' behavior according to some standard. Usually the standards learned at home form the basis for judgment. They also begin to think about how faith relates to life, and can discuss and explain what they believe. They may even begin to evaluate the validity of what they have been taught.

Susan, age ten, was asked how she feels when someone talks about God. She replied, "Weird, because I have a friend who talks about God a lot, but she's mean!" She defined sin as "something you do wrong and know is wrong when you did it." When asked what happens when a person dies, she answered, "Their soul goes someplace—there's no such thing as hell. If we're God's children why would he send us there?"

Susan was able to judge her friend's inconsistency between belief and action, and it bothered her. Sin is still concretely related to action but very real to her. She has begun to synthesize what she has learned about God with her own sense of justice, so that she critically evaluates what she has heard about hell and decides it does not exist.

What a child learns about the Bible during the school years undergirds an ongoing relationship with God. Even though an eight-year-old boy may not understand all the implications of what he reads and hears, Bible stories become loved and familiar as he studies them in an atmosphere of love and acceptance. Fear of misinterpretation should not keep us from teaching the Bible to him. His relationship to God should be dynamic, personal and constantly growing. Misinterpretations will be cleared up as he matures. Moreover, part of the beauty of Scripture is that it can be understood on many levels. A child who has no concept of God's wrath over evil may still learn that God loves animals, so he saved them from the flood. Tommy, with his story of the "good Americans," may have actually taken the first step in application by realizing that the "good guys" help people in need, even though he went overboard by declaring that "Americans are always the good guys."

Most children see God as a celestial rule-giver as well as a helper and friend. They also see adults as rule-givers. A school-age child is legalistic, and feels loved and secure when he or she knows firm limits are set on behavior (even though he or she may not always obey them). God's grace is a difficult, if not impossible, concept for school-age children to understand. Although they may offer and accept forgiveness, their natural inclination is to do something to make up for detected offenses in order to restore a damaged relationship. Undetected offenses usually cause a gnawing sense of guilt.

As reasoning ability increases, so does an attempt to allay guilt feelings. School-age children want and expect punishment for their wrongdoing. Younger children, if given the opportunity to choose their own punishment, will choose the one that hurts the most. Older children tend to choose punishments related to the offense, such as returning a stolen item and apologizing.[9] They may also begin to respond to rewards for good behavior more than to threats of punishment for disobedience.[10] Although ten-year-old Marti, quoted at the beginning of this chapter, could state unequivocally that she knows Jesus is her friend because he died on the cross for her sins, she will probably not realize the full meaning of her confession until late adolescence or early adulthood. Her view of sin is still based on her own violation of rules. She has no real insight into the problem of evil in the world and how sin separates us from God. She can recognize her own naughtiness, but she sees no connection between that and thieves and murderers, whom she considers the "really bad people."[11]

"Who Can Draw a Spirit?"

Gradually during the elementary school years, a child's understanding of God becomes more supernatural (Figures 22-25). By age twelve a boy or girl will probably understand the concept of God as Spirit, but may give you a scientific explanation of how that Spirit can pass through walls. When a class of twelve-year-olds was asked to draw a picture of God they responded, "That's dumb. Who can draw a Spirit?" and "That's impossible—no one knows what he looks like."

During ages nine through twelve, prayer is a private conversation with God about things not discussed with other people (Figure 25). Children at this age tend to pray more spontaneously in response to feelings (fear, anxiety, loneliness) as well as at routine times. Negative emotions motivate prayer more than positive feelings. Children who have easily prayed aloud in a group become self-conscious and hesitant as they approach adolescence. Prayers also become more altruistic as children become increasingly aware of and concerned about the world. Projects which involve them with children from other countries or cultures can be deeply meaningful, enabling them to pray for, correspond with and materially support someone in need.

Heroes strongly attract the older child. Biographies and novels about Christians who lived out their faith provide role models for decision making and behavior. A friend recently told me how influential a film about Martin Luther had been to her as a child. His statement before the Diet of Worms ("My conscience is captive to the Word of God. I cannot and will not recant, for to act against conscience is neither right nor safe. Here I stand. I can do no other!") became a model for her so that she was able to resist following the crowd when her conscience led her otherwise.

Missionary speakers challenge and excite older children, giving them a personal glimpse into countries they are studying in school. Many will be stimulated to study the history, geography and people of these countries. Some may want to become "pen pals" with a missionary or a child from another country.

School-age children make remarkable strides in six short years. Their world expands from the tight circle of their family to include children and adults in school, church and the community, and even people in other lands. They master enough basic intellectual skills to function in society, and learn that they are productive and increasingly independent persons. They grow in their understanding of God as Creator, lawgiver and friend through the teaching and example of parents, teachers and other adults. They develop an appreciation for rules and a conscience which bothers them when they disobey. By the end of the elementary school years children who have received religious instruction will be able to articulate their faith, and may even begin to question the validity of what they have been taught. Out of the relative stability and security of this "latency" period, they are now prepared to enter the storm of adolescence.

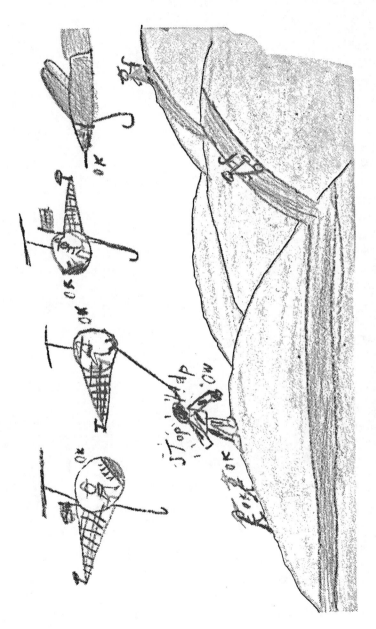

Figure 15/"The good Americans." Tommy, age 7

Figure 16/"God is everywhere. I love God and God loves me." Tami, age 6

Figure 17/"God is love."
Amanda, age 6

Figure 18/"God is happy. God makes
flowers grow. God makes
nice weather." Mark, age 7

Figure 19/"God made the flowers and grass." Sarah, age 7

Figure 20/"God wishes everybody a happy Valentine's Day."   Holly, age **7**

Figure 21/"He helps us."
Michael, age 7

Figure 22/"The outer ring is his power."
Kristin, age 8

Figure 23/"God is a spirit."   Patti, age 7

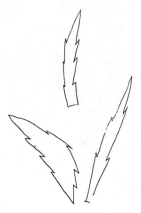

Figure 24/"God is like lightning."
Amy, age 8

Figure 25/"When I think of God I think of . . ."   Terri, age 11

Chapter Four
Testing the Truth: The Turbulent Teens
Judith Allen Shelly

The adolescent unit finally settled into an uncharacteristic calm at the 11 P.M. change of shift. Most of the patients seemed to be asleep. Then, the unmistakable sweet, pungent odor of marijuana drifted down the hall. The nurses guessed that Joe Weaver's room was the source of the smoke. The sixteen-year-old had been admitted the night before with multiple fractures and possible head injuries after an automobile accident. Prior to the accident, Joe had come home drunk. His parents lectured him sternly and sent him to his room. Joe climbed out his bedroom window and drove off in the family car. Unable to negotiate a curve, he slid off the road and crashed into a tree at sixty miles per hour.

"I guess all kids have to try their wings," Joe's mother told the nurses before she left. "He's probably just a normal teen-ager, but suddenly he's like a stranger living in our home."

Martha Young's parents were also concerned about her. She had been admitted for removal of a pilonidal cyst the next morning. A lively seventeen-year-old, Martha related well to the other teen-agers on the unit and was respectful and trusting of the nurses. She seemed to have a close relationship with her parents and was somewhat distressed that her mother was not allowed to stay overnight with her. Martha's parents stayed until visiting hours were over and shared family devotions (at their daughter's request) before they left. When they stopped by the nurses' station on their way out Mrs. Young remarked, "I'm a bit worried about Martha. It seems so abnormal for her to want me to stay. Aren't teen-agers supposed to rebel against their parents?"

The Move toward Independence

What do you think of when you hear the word *teen-ager?* Common word associations are *rebellious, drugs, wild* or *generation gap.* The usual stereotype of adolescents is negative and frightening to most adults, but it is not accurate. Certainly there are tensions between adults and teen-agers over beliefs, values, attitudes, opinions and lifestyle which result from the adolescents' growing sense of identity and independence, but the generation gap, as such, is a myth. Merton P. Strommen, in a 1970 survey of Lutheran youth, found that two contrasting groups of youth showed widely different attitudes. About 20 per cent were "peer oriented." They most resembled the common stereotype of teen-agers. They were critical of their churches and were unwilling to delay gratification of desires. The remaining 80 per cent were "broadly oriented" and related well to adults as well as to their contemporaries. In general, they shared the beliefs and values of their parents and the church.[1]

Strommen's findings were by no means unique. Havighurst and Keating quote numerous studies which show that most teen-agers hold the same religious beliefs as their parents. Most religious youth feel that they come from happy homes and give their parents credit for their religious beliefs. They usually assert their individuality by demanding to be heard, rather than by rebelling against authority.[2] A 1981 study by Nurses Christian Fellowship of 263 churched youth, ages thirteen to eighteen, also agreed.[3] Of those surveyed, 79.5 per cent felt that their beliefs were the same as, or similar to, their parents' beliefs. Only 12.5 per cent held very different beliefs, and most of those thought their own beliefs were stronger (for example, "My parents don't go to church" or "My parents only use God's name in curse words").

Teen-agers are quick to recognize inconsistencies between what adults teach and how they actually behave. They can become quickly disillusioned by hypocrites. Psychologist Arthur Jersild quotes studies which indicate that adolescents react in one of two ways to conflict between what parents say and do. The teen-ager will either cling desperately to a formal acceptance of ideals and religious convictions, or become cynical and reject their religious beliefs.[4]

During these years the peer group does become more significant than parents in influencing values; however, the values taught in earlier years will probably be maintained. Peers who share these values will be sought for close friendships. Adolescence is a turbulent time, a time of breaking away from the security of dependence and moving toward independence. Many are caught in the middle. During this insecure period of establishing identity apart from parents, the peer group provides a tenuous security. Dressing, talking and acting like their peers are essential to being accepted.

Adolescents can be extremely perceptive about their own behavior. They know how they affect parents and other adults. Many regret the tension but feel they must go through the motions of testing and trying, and occasionally rebelling. From teens surveyed by NCF the most common advice offered adults was "try to understand." A fourteen-year-old said, "Don't be so hard on teen-agers because it is the roughest part of their lives." A sixteen-year-old pleaded, "Try to understand everything a teen-ager has to go through and remember that you were teen-agers once and had to go through many of the same problems." A seventeen-year-old counseled, "Be patient. We're often unreasonable, but we try hard."

Tension Headache #28

Strommen identifies several areas in which there was the most disagreement between youth and adults surveyed. Even in these areas, however, the tension is neither static nor constant, nor is it necessarily a negative force.[5] The source of greatest tension was among youth who distrusted adults. Teen-agers who were anti-adult were also usually antichurch. These youth shared other common characteristics. They were generally unhappy with their families, liberal in theology, least likely to see their church as a reconciling community, least able to affirm a faith, most troubled with feelings of isolation and pressure, most separated from their parents, most given to personal gratification, most ardent advocates of social reform and least convinced of a Christian hope.

Another source of tension was the priority given to personal piety. Only 21 per cent of the youth in Strommen's survey maintained that Christian beliefs formed the foundation of their approach to life. Only 12 per cent reported reading the Bible daily or weekly, whereas 43 per cent of youth surveyed in 1959 and 1962 read the Bible regularly. A 1977-78 Gallup Poll, however, showed that a high proportion of teen-agers believe in a personal God and pray regularly, but only 25 per cent are very confident of organized religion. One-third consider themselves "very religious" but do not attend church.[6]

Unwillingness to delay gratification was a strong source of tension between youth and adults in Strommen's study. Just over a third (35 per cent) of the youth said they "have no moral reason for delaying an experience which will give them pleasure." Over half (55 per cent) agreed that a person ought to "enjoy what he can now and not wait." Adolescent unwillingness to practice restraint was measured by asking whether they had engaged in any of the following activities during the past year:

getting drunk (58 per cent)
swearing (89 per cent)
having sexual intercourse outside of marriage (37 per cent)
attending X-rated movies (72 per cent)
reading pornographic literature (64 per cent)

In addition, 25 per cent of the youth surveyed were "drug oriented" to some extent. A high correlation was evident between those who felt premarital sex was acceptable and those who were likely to use drugs. (Drug use has risen dramatically since the survey was taken in 1970 but now seems to be leveling off, according to a survey of high-school seniors by the National Institute on Drug Abuse.[7])

Another source of tension identified by Strommen was the tendency of youth to have strong positive feelings for people who are oppressed, shunned or condemned. They consistently expressed less prejudice than adults do (except toward people who embody a threatening ideology), but often their rhetoric was not transferred into action. They admitted to doing less than adults in actually performing specific acts of kindness. Other studies show that, in spite of adolescent idealism, teen-agers tend to be limited in their concern about social, political, economic and international issues.[8]

For some youth, alienation also created tension with adults. Teen-agers who felt alienated from other people also felt alienated from God. Alienation from life in general was also a problem for some youth. Feelings of pessimism were strongly tied to an adolescent's beliefs and values. Pessimistic youth were "alienated from Christian hope and the truth of the Christian gospel." Feelings of pressure and isolation were strongly associated with an unhappy family and with a concern over their relationship with God. Purposelessness seemed to be the culmination of pessimism, pressure and isolation. Strommen found that about 28 per cent of those he surveyed suffered this lack of meaning and purpose.

Focusing on the tensions between adults and adolescents can be frightening. It seems to confirm adult suspicions that teen-agers are "up to no good." Recent surveys about teen-age sexual activity, drug and alcohol use, and rejection of adult standards show increases in each area. In the meantime, teen-agers are pleading for understanding and support. One sixteen-year-old speaks for many when he says, "Don't judge all of us by a few of the bad ones. Give us each a chance to show you what we're like."

Havighurst and Keating have summarized the results of numerous studies on religious development and conclude that most adults would be surprised to discover what teen-agers are most concerned about. Adults tend to overestimate adolescent anxieties about family and sexual activities and underestimate their concerns about faith, values and life goals.[9]

What Adolescents Are Thinking

According to developmental psychologists, one of the major changes during adolescence is the development of abstract thought. Teens gain a new ability to understand analogies and symbols, to dream of an ideal world, to empathize and to philosophize. The process starts at about age twelve and continues to about age twenty.[10]

Younger children usually take biblical analogies literally, or misinterpret them to be personally meaningful. Six-year-old Tommy (p. 39) could understand the story of the good Samaritan ("good Americans") as the "good guys" rescuing a wounded man from the "bad guys" and realize that God wants us to be "good guys," but the parable takes on new meaning for an adolescent.

Lynn, age seventeen, was amazed when she realized the significance of Jesus' use of an outcast Samaritan for the good neighbor and the respectable religious leaders for the unloving hypocrites. Lynn looked pensive, then began to share her thoughts:

"There was this girl at school named Joan that I always tried to ignore because she was kind of weird. I didn't want my friends to see me hang around with her. Her parents were divorced just before she moved here last year and her Mom worked two jobs. She was never home, so Joan just hung around whoever was nice to her. She got in with a gang that was always shooting up with drugs and getting drunk. They told us in school this week that Joan overdosed on drugs and booze, and she died. Maybe if I hadn't been so worried about being popular myself, I could have been a 'good Samaritan' to Joan, and she might not have gotten in with that gang."

Not all adolescents develop abstract thinking, but most do. Some adults remain concrete thinkers. The NCF study asked teenagers, "Jesus compared the kingdom of heaven with a tiny mustard seed that grows into a big tree. What do you think he meant by that?" Most enjoyed the analogy, and some even proposed delightful elaborations about how beautiful heaven becomes as more and more people believe in Christ and enter it. A slight in-

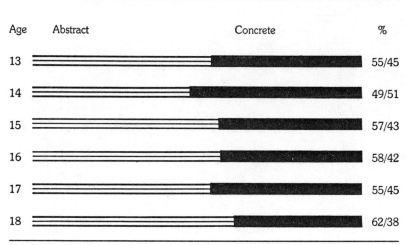

Age	Abstract	Concrete	%
13			55/45
14			49/51
15			57/43
16			58/42
17			55/45
18			62/38

Figure 26
NCF Study: Abstract vs. Concrete Thinking

crease in abstract thinking can be seen with age. The increase would probably be more pronounced if this had been a longitudinal study and the same individuals were tested for six consecutive years. Variables between age groups such as intelligence, educational methods experienced and family relationships were not controlled in our sampling.

Adolescents do not naturally outgrow concrete thinking. They need appropriate experience and instruction to develop more mature thought patterns.[11] Adults can encourage growth by stimulating adolescents to carefully consider various aspects of their faith and values, challenging them to move beyond the obvious. When Lynn's Sunday-school class first sat down to study Luke 10 they groaned and complained, "We've studied this passage a million times. Can't we move on to something exciting, like Daniel or Revelation?" It took patient prodding by their teacher to expand their understanding beyond what they already knew about the good Samaritan.

The process of learning to think maturely and abstractly is enhanced by a growing idealism. Teen-agers are able to conceive of

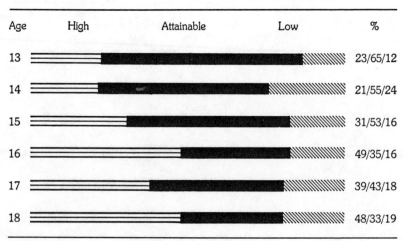

Age	High	Attainable	Low	%
13				23/65/12
14				21/55/24
15				31/53/16
16				49/35/16
17				39/43/18
18				48/33/19

Figure 27
NCF Study: Adolescent Idealism

a perfect society where there is no injustice or oppression, and they may become impatient with adults who are content to live with the existing order. Adolescents often dream of altruistic vocations, and in some periods of history have eagerly joined great causes to "save the world." Teen-agers are also beginning to imagine their ideal mate. They may develop crushes on teachers, coaches and pastors, only to be disillusioned when their idols do something which does not meet their ideal standards. Adolescents who were nurtured in the church might presumably also consider the qualities of an "ideal Christian," but our study showed a surprising lack of idealism when teens were asked, "What is your idea of an ideal Christian?"

Those rated as having "high ideals" of an ideal Christian gave examples such as Jesus or the pope, or described perfect obedience to God's will and unwavering love for other people. The "attainable ideals" category included those who listed the basic criteria for Christian faith, such as "someone who accepts Jesus Christ as Savior and tries to do his will." Those in the "low ideals" category gave answers which did not even meet basic criteria for being a Christian, such as "someone who goes to church occasionally" or "someone who tries to be nice to people."

Survey results leave more questions than answers. Are teenagers finding their heroes and role models in other areas, such as sports, television or popular music? Is there a general disillusionment left over from Watergate and Vietnam? The activism of the sixties seemed to fade into an egocentricity in the seventies, and the earlier tendency to glorify and romanticize leaders has changed to a spirit of disclosing corruption in high places. If idealism is on the wane, is this trend a hindrance or an advantage? It could foster the ability to set realistic goals and to understand that we are sinners saved by grace. On the other hand, it seems to be contributing to both an increasing pessimism among youth and a lack of inspiring role models.

Another dimension of abstract thinking which develops during adolescence is the ability to empathize. Children before the age of twelve can memorize the words of the golden rule and they may know they should not be mean to others, but they do not understand that other people have feelings as they do. Our survey asked, "What does the golden rule ('do unto others as you would have them do unto you') tell you to do if someone tells you that you look ugly?" Most were able to empathize well, with answers becoming more sophisticated and more deeply empathic as the respondents matured. One very perceptive eighteen-year-old answered, "People who say something like that must feel terrible about themselves. I'd try to find out what's really bothering them." Those judged unable to empathize gave answers such as "I'd kick him in the teeth" or "I'd tell him to consider the source."

The ability to philosophize and to think logically are also dimensions of abstract thought. Younger children can accept two opposing ideas as true at the same time. Teen-agers develop an ability to question illogical statements and speculate about their meaning. Adolescents surveyed were asked to consider the following syllogism:

1. God loves all people.

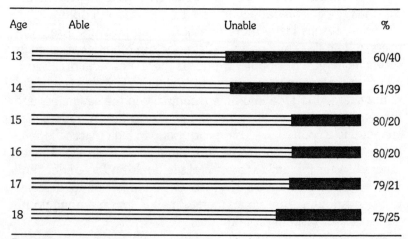

Age	Able	Unable	%
13			60/40
14			61/39
15			80/20
16			80/20
17			79/21
18			75/25

Figure 28
NCF Study: Ability to Empathize

2. The world is filled with starving people.

3. If God really loves people, he would not let them starve.

They were then asked whether they agreed with the logic, and to explain why if they disagreed. Most were able to recognize flaws in the logic. Explanations ranged from "people are starving because we don't share what we have" and "we cause people to starve when we don't help them—it is not God's fault" to "people are starving because they worship cows instead of eating them."

Appearances Are Deceiving

Heidi, age fourteen, blossomed on the church youth retreat. She enjoyed the Bible studies and was able to overcome shyness enough to openly share her spiritual concerns with her small group. She glowed with enthusiasm. When she got home she slumped into a chair, dumping her gear in a heap. "How was the retreat?" her mother asked. Heidi mumbled that the pancakes were cold and that the boys made so much noise she could not sleep, then went to her room and closed the door.

Havighurst and Keating report that the adult image of the re-

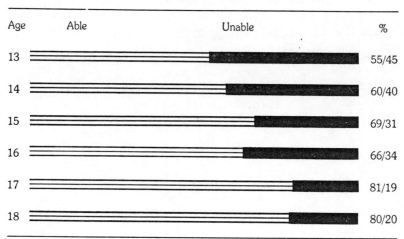

Figure 29
NCF Study: Ability to Philosophize

ligious concerns and values of youth tends to be one of "hedging and drifting." They often fear their children will reject their heritage.[12] But a parent may not see what is actually going on inside an adolescent. Teen-agers are naturally introspective. They can spend hours thinking about their own thoughts, writing secrets in diaries or composing poetry about their feelings. They often seem obsessed with keeping their thoughts private, especially from parents, but also from peers. Adolescents feel emotions with great intensity, and often perceive their feelings as unique and special. They frequently do not share their thoughts because they are afraid that no one could possibly understand.[13]

Contrary to appearances, there is no revolution in attitude toward religion, or even in religious beliefs and activities during adolescence.[14] Of adolescents surveyed by NCF, 98.5 per cent expressed a strong belief in God. About half said that their beliefs about God had changed since becoming a teen-ager, but 81 per cent of those said their faith had become stronger, more mature or more relevant. Most attributed the change to catechetical instruction, Bible study, youth camps and programs, and the influence of peers and Christian leaders.

Although the Gallup Poll found the general youth population disillusioned with the institutional church, the NCF study (of pri-

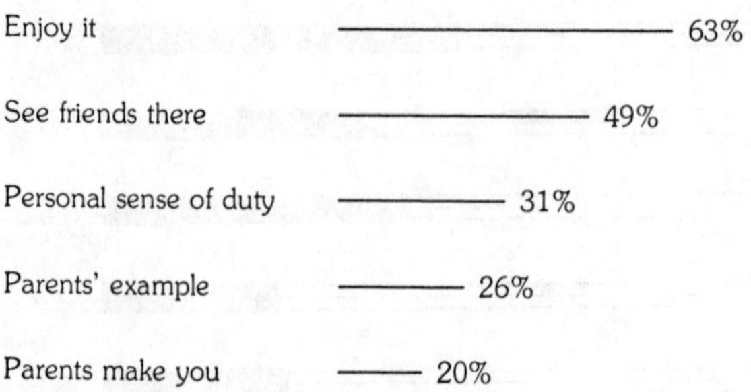

Enjoy it	———————— 63%
See friends there	——————— 49%
Personal sense of duty	———— 31%
Parents' example	——— 26%
Parents make you	—— 20%

Figure 30
NCF Study: Reasons for Church Involvement

marily churched adolescents) showed that 72 per cent of those surveyed attend church services often. Only 6 per cent never attend. Most continue to attend Sunday school and participate in church activities during high school. The primary reason for church involvement given by most teens surveyed was that they enjoy it. Very few attended because of parental pressure alone. Of the 20 per cent who said they are involved in church activities because their parents make them go, most also listed other reasons, including that they enjoy it.

André Godin, a French psychologist-priest, defined five developmental features of spiritual development which take place during adolescence.[15] First, a historical consciousness is awakened, which leads to an ability to discover God's plan in history. Younger children have little sense of history. Seven-year-old Donna was asked if she knew who started the church. She replied, "Yes, Mr. and Mrs. Johnson [the sextons] did, because they are always here." During adolescence the concept of God's involvement with his people over the centuries and an eschatological perspective can become meaningful and even exciting. Teenagers are fascinated with "the end of the world" and apocalyptic literature.

Second, a symbolic function is developed. This transition from concrete to abstract thought gives the adolescent a new theological perspective. Younger children view symbolic practices literally. Six-year-old Kathy giggled when she saw her mother taking Communion. Asked why she was laughing Kathy replied, "Because you're drinking blood out of a toy glass." Teen-agers begin to understand the meaning of the sacraments, as well as of symbolic art and literature. They enjoy being able to interpret traditional Christian symbols and can be challenged to create their own symbols. The writings of C. S. Lewis and J. R. R. Tolkien may help expand their understanding of theological concepts through symbolic interpretations.

Third, a magical and superstitious mentality is progressively transformed into a mature prayer life. Some researchers note a disillusionment with prayer among adolescents because they recognize that God does not always answer prayer according to their wishes.[16] Young children often view devotional practices and sacraments as magical rites. They are concerned with using proper formulas and may become distraught if routine devotional practices are omitted. Jackie, age seven, ate a pickle off his dinner plate before the blessing was said. While his father prayed Jackie opened his mouth wide because "I wanted to make sure the pickle got blessed too." Up to age twelve most children see prayer as a means of obtaining material and psychological advantages.[17] According to the NCF study, teen-agers tend to see prayer as communication with God, their faithful friend and heavenly confidant.

Fourth, moralism is progressively reduced into a growing understanding of God's grace. Godin claims that this is very different from the simple development of a moral conscience, described by developmental psychologists such as Piaget and Kohlberg. Rather than the natural perceptions of what is right and wrong, the moralism which is taught to young children often becomes confused with Christianity. When coupled with the natural guilt feelings over an awakening sexuality and a tenuous self-concept, the adolescent may become preoccupied with asking God for forgiveness but never feeling forgiven. In order to move adolescents toward spiritual maturity, adults need to emphasize God's unmerited forgiveness at a time when they are strongly tempted to preach morality instead.

Fifth, Christian beliefs are continuously purified beyond the ambiguity of parental images. This paves the way to faith in Christ and a commitment in response to his Word. Godin's criterion for Christian maturity is "the distance it maintains from the psychological traits of a purely human religiosity."[18] As discussed in previous chapters, a child models his or her images of God upon parents and other significant adults. Even though school-age children begin to separate God from their parents, they continue to associate God's love, trustworthiness and willingness to forgive with the way their parents relate to them. Even many adults are left with an overwhelming bitterness toward God because of child-hood experiences with overly rigid or abusive parents. In late adolescence the maturity of moving beyond parental images of God can be stimulated and encouraged, enabling a young person to freely center his or her faith in God, as revealed in Scripture.

A maturing view of God is demonstrated in the NCF survey. Only 1.5 per cent of the teen-agers surveyed described God in anthropomorphic terms. Most described him according to charac-ter traits or functions. To the overwhelming majority, God is per-sonal, benevolent and very close. Only 4.5 per cent felt he is

"A friend," "My very best friend," "Like a trusted friend"	19%
"He loves me," "He loves everyone"	16%
"A Father," "My loving heavenly Father"	14%
"A helper," "He helps me," "Helps us when we are in trouble"	14%
"He is always there . . . (to help, to listen, to guide)"	13%
"He is my Savior," "He saves me"	11%
"Someone I can always go to"	11%
"He cares about me," "He comforts me"	11%
"He is my counselor/teacher/guide"	9%
"He is merciful," "He forgives me"	8%

Figure 31
NCF Study: What Is God Like to You? (top ten answers)

distant, vague or "like he's not there." Less than 1 per cent mentioned any characteristics pertaining to judgment or punishment (of these respondents, none was older than fourteen). Samplings from the East, Midwest and West show no significant difference in their views of God. Because older studies show greater concern about God's wrath, we are left to wonder how much influence culture and education might have on our concepts of God.

The survey also asked if they had experienced a serious illness since age thirteen and, if so, how it affected their thinking about God. Thirty-three said they had experienced a serious illness;

Attitudes	86%
Behavior	82%
Ability to forgive others	81%
Life goals	79%
Your personality	74%
Choice of friends	73%
Ability to love	72%
Sense of hope	70%
Whom you marry	69%
Sources of guidance	69%
Sense of meaning and purpose	68%
Concerns about death	65%
How you spend your time	64%
Fears and anxieties	64%
Guilt feelings	62%
Career plans	56%
How you spend your money	56%
Courses you take in school	34%
Sports you play	24%
None of the above	2%

Figure 32
NCF Study: A Person's Faith Should Affect . . .

64 per cent of them reported that the illness drew them closer to God and made them more sure of their faith. Only 12 per cent reported a negative effect ("I thought God hated me" or "I didn't think it was fair"). The others felt that their illness had no effect on their relationship with God, or were not sure.

Although studies conflict about the influence of religious beliefs on moral behavior and everyday life,[19] most teen-agers in the NCF survey felt that their faith should and did affect a wide range of attitudes and behaviors. They felt that there was a high correlation between what they thought their faith should affect and what it actually did affect, but several commented that they are not as consistent as they would like to be. Interestingly enough, only a small percentage thought their faith should affect the sports they play, even though in at least one sampling (which did not differ significantly from the others) a great deal of emphasis had been placed on teaching good sportsmanship as a fruit of Christian faith.

Strommen's 1963 study on Lutheran youth showed that "religious activity and cognitive beliefs in themselves are quite unrelated to much or little involvement in questionable or immoral practices."[20] He did find a strongly positive relationship between moral behavior and the religious climate of the home. He also found a correlation between "personal dedication" of youth, as revealed by their earnestness in religious practices, and their moral behavior. Zuck and Getz repeated Strommen's study on evangelical youth in 1968 with similar results.[21] In other words, parents should not expect the church, Sunday school or Christian schools to shape their teen-agers' moral behavior. Moral teaching starts at a very young age in the home. Parents teach morals by their own examples, and by openly and consistently discussing Christian values with their children.

"Try to Understand Us"

Adolescents are an enigma. They cry for attention, but reject it when it is given. They often show affection for adults they admire by hurling insults at them because their positive emotions embarrass them. They may reveal deep spiritual concerns, then become giddy and silly and deny they ever felt that way. They may try your patience to the utmost, then express gratitude for the limits you set.

Godin states, "Many investigators call attention to the reactional factor in adolescence which leads the young to reject the traditional God. He is simultaneously the God of their parents and the God of psychological projections which result from parental relationships."[22] We have seen that most adolescents do not really reject God, or even the beliefs and values of their parents; yet, in order to accomplish a normal developmental task, they must move out of the security of unquestioned acceptance of their parents' views into Christian maturity which involves a firsthand relationship with God. The transition is not always easy, for either adolescents or their parents. The beliefs and values of peers must be processed and evaluated, and sometimes tried, before an

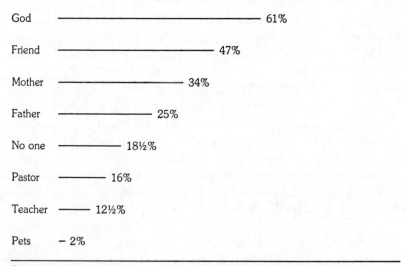

God	——————————————— 61%
Friend	———————————— 47%
Mother	——————— 34%
Father	———— 25%
No one	—— 18½%
Pastor	— 16%
Teacher	— 12½%
Pets	– 2%

Figure 33
NCF Study: When You Have Doubts and Questions about Your Faith,
Whom Do You Talk To?

adolescent's faith can become personal and solid.

Adults can easily be tempted to give up trying to assist a teen-ager spiritually, but to do so leaves him or her in a frightening position. Teen-agers do want to communicate with adults, but they want to be heard as well as to hear. They do not usually appreciate "advice" or "preaching," but they do want honest answers to their questions. They want understanding and compassion, even when they are not able to reciprocate.

Although a friend is the first person to whom teen-agers may go with doubts and questions about their faith, God is by far their most popular confidant. Mothers also rate fairly high. Some youth also go to fathers, pastors and teachers. A few feel comfortable only when talking to their pets. Asked what they want the person to do for them, a surprising majority said, "Answer my question" or "Show me some alternatives." Many wanted help in thinking through their problem, and a listening ear. Some wanted the person to pray for them.

Teen-agers surveyed were also asked why they avoid going to some people for help. The most common answer was "They wouldn't understand" (31 per cent), followed by "They might not approve and would reject me" (28 per cent) and "I'd be too embarrassed" (24 per cent). Others would avoid people who did not live the faith they professed, people they did not like and people they feared would betray their confidence. An adolescent's introspective nature, accentuated by a low self-image and a concern that his or her feelings are unique, may lead to alienation from the people who care most and would like to help. Adults can sometimes break through this isolation by gently identifying what a teen-ager seems to be feeling and suggesting that others share these concerns.

The spiritual needs of adolescents are closely tied to their need to accomplish developmental tasks. Erikson identifies their primary task as establishing "identity versus role confusion."[23] A maturing adolescent must endure the turbulence of casting off old, secure ways of thinking, acting and relating in order to become a mature person with a secure identity. The process of testing the truth of beliefs and values is important in establishing a mature faith and an ethical stance, but it is painful to the adolescent, as well as to parents and other caring adults.

Perhaps the best advice for dealing with teen-agers comes from the youth themselves. The NCF survey concluded with an opportunity to offer advice to adults. Here is a summary of the most frequently given advice. We'll let them have the last word: "Try to understand us. Listen when we talk and try to communicate with us. Give us more freedom. Trust us, respect us; don't assume all teen-agers are bad. Set limits and discipline us fairly when we disobey. Show love constantly and consistently. Don't preach at us—it only turns us off. Give encouragement and affirmation when we do things right. Don't condemn us and make us feel guilty. Spend time with us. Pray for us and with us. Be good examples for us. Lead (don't push) us in the right way. Don't yell and make threats, it only causes rebellion. Explain things so we don't get curious and find out in other ways."

Part II
Spiritual Assessment & Intervention

Each child is unique. Each comes from a different family background, a particular religious upbringing and a unique set of life experiences. Each child stands at his or her own special place in spiritual development. When a child's illness rudely interrupts life, the process of spiritual growth may be accelerated or it may be attenuated. A nurse may facilitate the spiritual growth of children and their families by encouraging them to verbalize their doubts and fears to God, and to continue family devotional practices. The resources of self, prayer, Bible reading and referral to the clergy can be adapted for use with children and their families after careful assessment by a nurse.

Spiritual needs are not always easy to recognize in children. They are often so integrated with more obvious physical and emotional needs that they do not appear at first glance to be spiritual. Dianne Stannard examines the spiritual aspects of some expressions of needs by children, and illustrates how nursing intervention can facilitate spiritual growth.

Judith Van Heukelem applies the nursing process to spiritual assessment and intervention. She gives guidelines for data collection and for making the nursing diagnosis. She also considers the importance of developmental levels.

Illness often distorts a person's view of God. When a young child already holds an immature concept of God, the problem can be especially distressing. Jack Rodgers, a chaplain in a children's hospital, examines some of the common misperceptions of God he has encountered among sick children and their families. He gives examples from his own experience of how unhealthy views of God increased the pain of those suffering, and how he gently nudged them into a fuller understanding of God.

Joseph Bayly writes about the suffering of children from first-hand experience as well as from the perspective of a theologian. He is the father of six children, three of whom died in childhood. His advice is perceptive and practical.

Ministering to dying children and their families is especially difficult for most nurses. Children are not supposed to die. It is not fair. It is a threat to everything that seems secure. Mae Shirley Cook approaches the problem as a coordinator of a Sunday-school program in a children's hospital. Between Sundays she visits the children who attended the classes. She gives her heart, as well as her time and talent, to the children. She supports the families of dying children and often attends the funeral and visits them after the death. She feels the pain with the families. She writes candidly about the difficulties involved in caring for a dying child, and offers helpful suggestions.

After reading about spiritual assessment and intervention, you may feel overwhelmed and inadequate. The authors speak from long experience and with expertise developed over the years. Susan Reed felt overwhelmed as a new graduate; she shares how she is overcoming her feelings of inadequacy. She gives some guidelines for avoiding the problems of discouragement and disillusionment, and provides positive resources for growth as a Christian nurse and communicates that spiritual care is an art which takes time, prayer and perseverance to develop.

Chapter Five
Recognizing Spiritual Needs

Dianne Stannard

Jan is ten years old. She had a craniotomy two days ago to remove a cystic tumor which had recurred. Tonight she was in a great deal of pain. Her head throbbed and her shoulder hurt. I medicated Jan with Tylenol #3 every three to four hours as ordered, but at 10:00 P.M. she was still restless and uncomfortable. When I entered the room to check her intravenous drip, she was crying out, "Lord, have mercy!" as she thrashed in the bed. Her mother tried to comfort her by rubbing her neck and talking softly to her. I said, "Jan, I think the Lord *will* have mercy." I asked her mother if Jan usually said prayers before bed and she said yes. Then her mother and I prayed for Jan while I rubbed Jan's neck. In five minutes Jan was asleep.

As a nurse who has worked with pediatric patients for several years, I have had numerous experiences with children and their families in times of crisis. Through these experiences I have become convinced that during the crisis of illness children not only have physical, emotional and psychosocial needs, but also very real spiritual needs. Before spiritual needs can be assessed, however, they must be defined. In 1 Corinthians 13 we read that "faith, hope, love abide." To these three I add forgiveness to constitute the spiritual needs I have identified.

Faith: The Risk of Trusting

A person who has faith in God is at peace and able to trust other people. A sense that "things will be all right" pervades. Without faith a person is fearful and anxious. A child's relationship with parents and other adults in authority is foundational to developing faith in God. If a child learns that significant adults can be trusted, trust in God's faithfulness usually comes naturally.

Ten-year-old Peter, however, found trust a risky business. He needed to receive blood as part of his chemotherapy. He was visibly upset, screaming, "I don't want someone else's blood!" When I asked him why, he said, "I just don't! What if it's some Japanese blood? Then my eyes will look funny!" I assured him that blood does not change a person's looks. He countered, "How do you know? Have you ever had a transfusion?" I had to admit that I had never received blood, but that I had seen many children who had, and that they did not look any different afterward.

"But what if that's a girl's blood? I don't want any old girl's blood!" The unknown results of a transfusion made him more and more anxious. I explained about the different types of blood and how his was matched with the blood he would receive. I said the only thing the blood would do was give him more blood cells to make him stronger, until his body could make more of its own. The mother of one of his roommates told Peter she had had a transfusion and was just fine after it. Finally, Peter allowed me to begin the transfusion. Forty-five minutes later, he was asleep.

Hope: Encouragement to Keep Going

People with hope are positive and optimistic. Without hope, negativism and depression ensue. George's case is a good example.

George had Hirschsprung's disease, which required numerous surgical procedures to correct the problem. At age nine he was admitted with adhesions of the bowel, necessitating yet another operation. Most of all, George hated the naso-gastric tube. He could cope with intravenous feedings and having blood drawn, but the N/G tube was more than he could tolerate. On the second day after surgery, when the tube is usually removed, George still had no bowel sounds so it had to remain in place. The talkative, smiling boy became sullen, refused to answer questions, frowned and cried.

Several days passed, but still no bowel sounds. George was very depressed, yet "keep the tube in" was the doctors' only choice. His mother tried to humor him, kept after him to answer questions, joked and bantered—no change in his outlook. On the sixth evening, I told George, "You must really be depressed and angry to have to keep that tube in your nose for so long. I don't blame you at all for not talking to anybody. It must be a pretty helpless feeling, not knowing when it will come out."

"Yes, it is." That was his first verbal response in days.

"The doctors feel pretty helpless too," I said. "They want to take out the tube as soon as possible. We all hope we can remove it soon."

Later that evening I talked with George's mother about his feelings. She became less demanding of him and that night he participated in their daily Bible reading and prayer, which he had not done since the surgery.

Love: A Sense of Belonging

Love brings a sense of self-worth and dignity, a sense of belonging. A child who does not feel loved is apt to feel lonely and alienated. An encounter with Mary clearly showed me how a hospitalized child can become isolated and alienated.

One evening thirteen-year-old Mary, a patient with cystic fibrosis, asked if she could talk with me. The floor was in chaos and all nurses were very concerned about another girl with cystic fibrosis. Susan, eight years old, had cor pulmonale and been critically ill for several days. Mary often talked with Susan, but I did not know if she realized how critical Susan's condition was. It was 11:30 before I could take time to talk with Mary.

"How come everyone around here knows Susan's going to die and none of you would tell me?" I felt guilty. Of course she had the right to know. We had been trying to protect her; instead we denied her the opportunity to share her feelings with us, isolating her when she desperately needed to talk to someone. I had avoided Mary, making myself look busy while in her room, hoping she would not ask questions and trying to deny to both of us the inevitability of Susan's death. I had ignored Mary's attempts to reach out—her hanging out around the nurses' station, her loud talk to attract attention, her unusual sullen silence.

We talked a long time. I admitted my feelings to Mary and shared with her my belief that Susan was in the Lord's hands, that he loved Susan far more than any of us could and that if Susan died I would see her again in heaven. Then we cried together, sharing our loss.

Forgiveness: Lifting the Burden

Without forgiveness, a child will be burdened with guilt, making it even harder to handle a crisis. Eight-year-old Billy was docile during his hospital stay. I had tried to get him involved in activities, but he held back and said very little.

One day he asked, "Why do I have cystic fibrosis? Is it because I am bad?" His mother and I assured Billy that he was in no way responsible, that he was born with the disease just as some of the children on the floor were born with heart problems and that God doesn't punish children by making them sick. From then on Billy was better able to verbalize his feelings.

Faith, hope, love and forgiveness—children and their families are apt to experience any or all of these four spiritual needs during an illness. These needs are expressed verbally and nonverbally; subtly and blatantly. By looking at verbal and nonverbal clues we may tune in to spiritual needs. Through further communication and examination, we may confirm those diagnoses and become more equipped to meet those needs.

A Family Affair
Spiritual needs of parents should be given first priority. After assessing their needs it is often easier to understand their child's needs. If we are able to help the parents, they will be better able to support their child.

The parents' faith is tested the moment their child is admitted to the hospital. Five-year-old Jerry had been admitted to the treatment room with grand mal seizures. Recurrent brain tumors had been removed and his mother knew that further surgical intervention was impossible. She paced back and forth outside the room, waiting for some word on her son's condition. In the midst of the crisis no nurse could take time to talk at length with Mrs. Wilson, but I paused long enough to explain what the doctors were doing and to give her some hope that the seizures could be stopped.

She asked, "Dianne, what would you do if that were your child in there?"

"I would pray . . . and I am praying," I replied. Then I was called away to perform other tasks. When I next saw her she was much less anxious, talking quietly with her husband in Jerry's room.

Fear and anxiety are common in a strange environment, and are compounded by surgical procedures, hospital policies, complicated tests, medical terminology and possible diagnoses. Parents sometimes express their feelings by demanding, "What are you going to do?" "When will we know the results?" "Is his temperature normal?" Parents may sound hostile or aggressive in an attempt to control a situation which frightens them. They may say, "We demand to see the doctor now!" or "You are *not* going to awaken her!" or "The light has been on for five minutes and nobody has bothered to answer it." Other parents readily admit their feelings by saying, "I know I'm asking a lot of questions, but I'm so anxious" or "I'm really afraid of what the doctors might find."

Nonverbal clues of fear and anxiety are numerous. Chain smoking, pacing the halls, overeating (or fasting) and insomnia are common signs of parents' lack of faith or faith at its lowest ebb.

The problem of parental guilt is widespread. "Why didn't I notice that knot on her leg sooner?" "Why wasn't I watching him more closely?" "What did I do to make my baby be born like this?" Because parents feel guilty about their child's illness, they may be overly protective, fulfilling their child's every wish. Such children and their parents make frequent demands and tax the patience of the care-givers, making it difficult to create a therapeutic relationship between hospital staff, patient and family.

When a child is critically ill, parents usually feel helpless and hopeless. "They've done all they can," they say. "The doctor said there are no more drugs to try." "I feel like an ant that's about to be stepped on." Parents may cry, or even withdraw from others. Hopelessness may lead to loneliness and alienation: "Nobody understands what I'm going through." "There's nobody I can turn to." At this point the parents may not be communicating with each other, visitors and calls may be refused and sleep (to escape thinking of their child's suffering and possible death) may be their primary activity.

Sally Jenkins was a two-year-old with rhabdomyosarcoma who was hospitalized for several months. After diagnostic tests a tumor was removed from her right lower abdomen, along with her right kidney. Sally developed infections, a fistula and later had metastases to the brain, which caused seizures. Though the family lived ninety miles away, her mother stayed with her constantly because Sally would scream unless her mother provided all her care. Mr. Jenkins worked full time, took courses at a junior college and spent much of his time with his parents, who were caring for Sally's four-year-old sister; he came to the hospital infrequently.

During the second month of Sally's hospitalization Mrs. Jenkins began to smoke, which she had not done in years. She ate more and more, bringing potato chips, candy and desserts into her daughter's room on the pretense of coaxing Sally to eat them. Soon many of the woman's clothes no longer fit. When her husband called each day, she was abrupt and angry. She complained to me, "He doesn't know what it's like to sit here day after day and watch her suffer. He doesn't care." During one weekend visit she would not talk to him at all. I consulted a social worker, who counseled the couple. Finally they were able to share their mutual and individual concerns. Mr. Jenkin's mother came to stay with Sally so Mrs. Jenkins could go home for several days. Mr. Jenkins made more frequent and longer visits to the hospital as Sally's condition deteriorated. Finally, we arranged for both parents to stay at the hospital during the last week of Sally's life.

We of the health care professions must recognize these verbal and nonverbal clues with which parents express spiritual needs. When nonverbal clues are noted, a nurse can try to draw out parents and encourage verbalization. With verbal clues, rephrase what is being said and encourage feedback. We can look at clues and hypothesize that a parent has a certain need but, as in all good nursing care, we must obtain all the facts in order to be most effective in alleviating problems.

Kid Stuff

A child may be expressing in actions or in words the needs the parents have identified. Or, a completely different spiritual need may be present.

Fear and anxiety in hospitalized children have been widely discussed, though not usually as spiritual needs. As is true for their parents, this is the most readily identifiable clue to a spiritual need. When a boy screams, cries and tries to escape from you, he obviously does not have faith or trust in you. Perhaps his faith in a loving God is equally shaky, especially if his parents are visibly anxious.

Even infants can sense when the people holding them are anxious. Older children quickly perceive tension in parental actions, words or tone of voice. They are not easily deceived by assurances that all will be well. If a hospital and its procedures are strange to an adult, they are even more strange to a child: "What are you going to do?" "Are you going to give me a shot?" "I want my mama!" A barrage of questions (sometimes a stalling technique), nervous giggling, regressive behavior, compulsive routines and insomnia are also possible indications of anxiety.

Molly, age fifteen, had to have many diagnostic tests including enemas and a sigmoidoscopy. Whenever we prepared her for the tests she would giggle and pretend not to pay attention. Her mother, however, expressed appreciation that we explained things beforehand and said that Molly was less anxious when she knew about a procedure. Things were different, though, with six-year-old Arnold, who had never been in a hospital before. He would become hysterical whenever someone came to take a blood sample or insert an intravenous needle. He screamed. He yelled, "You're killing me!" He bit and scratched. It was very traumatic for him . . . and for the nurses.

Teen-age Cindy was always concerned about her appearance during each of her frequent hospitalizations. She had a special way of fixing her hair, and when she had to have an oxygen face mask she would remove the mask often, fluff up her hair and then carefully replace the mask. She was afraid she would look ugly, so when she grew too weak to do it herself we would fluff her hair for her each time we removed the mask.

When Kelly's mother would leave for the night, the two-year-old would lie in her crib and howl, waking up the other children. Cuddling her, trying to give her something to eat and dosing her with chloral hydrate only made her scream more. During the second night of her insomnia I tried numerous tactics and finally got her to sleep by pushing her around the halls in her stroller. The motion and security of her stroller contributed to a quiet night for the ward.

Children are also apt to experience feelings of guilt when ill. Many children think that illnesses are punishments for misdeeds. A child who feels guilty may act like an ideal patient—the little boy who never complains or cries, the school-age girl who co-operates with every procedure, the teen-ager who never asks questions. Some say things such as "My mother told me I couldn't go swimming, but I went anyway and now I'm sick" or "My father will be so angry that I'm in the hospital again."

When I was a child, I had a perforated eardrum. Every week for months I had to undergo the painful procedure of having an old patch removed from my eardrum and a new one applied. I dreaded the office visit, but tried hard not to cry while the doctor worked on my ear. I felt that it was my punishment for diving off the high diving board when I was not supposed to. So I silently did penance when I wanted to scream.

Lack of hope may produce depression in children. A child who is cheerful and outgoing may become overly quiet and withdrawn; a normally quiet child may become almost mute. They say, "Just leave me alone" or "I don't want to talk to you" or "I want to go home." When children know they are going home, they almost always feel more hopeful and become less withdrawn.

If a child is lonely and alienated he or she may misbehave to receive attention, acting belligerent or demanding. Others withdraw. Many coping behaviors overlap. We must continually delve into the feelings behind a child's actions or statements in order to assess spiritual needs. Parents can be helpful because they know their child's personality and are able to detect unusual behavior. Some children confide in their parents when they do not feel free to confide in others. Many, however, try to spare their parents hurt by keeping hidden their fears, depression, guilt and alienation. Each family is different. Each child is different. All of their needs change from day to day.

We must pick up the clues parents and children send out and recognize potential areas of need. By being alert to these possible needs, by asking leading questions and by following up on feedback, we may do much to meet a child's spiritual needs.

Chapter Six
Assessing the Spiritual Needs of Children & Their Families

Judith Van Heukelem

Appropriate intervention in spiritual care requires sound assessment. Most nurses sense that the spiritual dimension is important to children and their families, but have had little direction or encouragement to include it in routine nursing assessments. A common temptation is to use intuition or a "sixth sense" to determine spiritual needs.

There are two potential hazards in the intuitional approach. First, intuition is based largely on our own experience; therefore, it has limited parameters. I easily bring my own orientation into someone else's situation. Second, we may be unconsciously meeting our own needs in the name of patient care. Our needs can range from feeling that we must evangelize to avoiding the discomfort of talking about personal religious beliefs (or lack of beliefs). Consequently, we must base our intervention on assessment that is both systematic and objective.

Knowing what to look for and looking in an orderly manner are keys to systematic assessment. In the physical care of a kidney patient a nurse knows what is normal (clear, amber urine) and abnormal (cloudy, bloody urine), and periodically checks the catheter drainage bag for signs. In the spiritual dimension, we need as well to know cardinal signs of healthy and unhealthy spirituality.[1] (See also chapter seven.) Objective assessments are verifiable and reproducible by another professional with comparable experience and skill. For example, a nurse might say of an adult with a chronic debilitating disease, "I believe Mr. Smith has a spiritual need. He isn't eating, doesn't sleep well and says that he doesn't know why God allows him to keep on living. He said he's 'just taking up space and energy.' I think he lacks meaning and purpose in his life." Such a statement is based on solid evidence.

If sound assessment is crucial to caring for adults, it is even more important in the pediatric setting. Children, especially young children, have a limited ability to communicate, particularly about abstract concepts. In addition, we must be sensitive to the rights of parents to influence their own children. Rushing in could be damaging as well as inappropriate. We must understand the total situation before intervening spiritually with a pediatric patient; consequently, it makes sense to use the nursing process. The steps, as described by Aspinall, are:

1. Data collection (gathering information)
2. Nursing diagnosis (identifying the problem)
3. Plan for nursing action (selecting an approach)
4. Implementation of plan (carrying out the approach)
5. Evaluation of effectiveness (checking the consequences)[2]

The first two steps of the nursing process (data collection and nursing diagnosis) constitute the assessment phase. These steps warrant special attention.

Watching for Clues, Listening for Cries

A nurse begins data collection by gathering any available background information. Sources include a patient's chart, doctors, referral sheets and other team members' observations. In addition, specific questions can be asked while taking a nursing history. For example, you could ask a child the following questions:

1. How do you feel when you're in trouble?
2. Who do you turn to when you're scared? (If the answer is, "my parents," ask who else.)
3. What are favorite things you like when you're happy? when you're sad?
4. Who do you like to talk to when you're happy? sad? lonely?
5. Do you know who God is? What is he like?
6. Do you ever pray? How does God answer your prayers?
7. What do you think dying is like?[3]

A pediatric nurse gathering data regarding spiritual needs must watch for cues which will contribute to the nursing diagnosis. Nonverbal cues alone are rarely enough to form a conclusive diagnosis, but they are helpful in understanding the overall picture of the spiritual needs and resources of a child or family member. Parents may send nonverbal cues in their body language such as slumped posture, behavior such as crying, or types of reading material, radio or television programs. Children also speak volumes with body language, whether pensive, withdrawn or overly cheerful. Behavior indicating possible spiritual needs includes nightmares, refusal to participate in hospital school programs and morbid curiosity about other children's illnesses. A teen-age boy with cystic fibrosis was found browsing in the chart of another cystic fibrosis patient who had just died. The alert nurse who discovered him looked beyond her immediate concerns for loss of confidentiality and intrusion into the nurses' station to his possible questions and fears.

Reading materials and leisure activities that a child prefers can also yield important information. In addition, the kind of greeting cards and visitors received tells a lot about a child's support system and whether spiritual influences are present.

Verbal cues give much more definitive help in assessing spiritual needs and resources. Parents may make passing statements about their own beliefs, struggles or support system. Twelve-year-old Jenny lay in serious condition with degenerative myopathy of the heart. Her parents said, "We're trying to figure out the reason for this. How can it be God's will?" Parents are more likely to share deep concerns in a relaxed atmosphere. At times, the best thing to do is to invite one or both parents with you on your coffee break, and simply listen attentively.

Children's statements can be covertly or overtly indicative of spiritual concerns. Some are general and occur during playtime, such as references to church, Sunday school, Bible stories, death or God. Others are more specific, even blatant. Jeanette, age ten, was admitted for the second time with abdominal pain of unknown origin. She told a nurse who took the time to sit and listen, "I just don't know why I still have so much pain. I thought for a while that God was mad at me and was punishing me for something."

Timing can be extremely important. Kikuchi feels the key is being available "at critical times, in case the child wants to talk, and then being sensitive in picking up indirect cues designed to test reactions."[4] Bedtime and nighttime can be difficult for hospitalized children. Their defenses are down and their anxieties are up.

One evening was very tense for the pediatric unit in which I worked. A child was in critical condition after having a cardiac arrest early that day. All the children knew her and sensed that things were grave. Near the end of the shift I went into one of the rooms where I discovered that Gail, age eleven, and Karen, age eight, were wide awake. Gail suddenly said to me, "I wish Sister Marie was here. She was my primary school teacher, and she really meant a lot to me. She would understand!"

Karen slipped out of bed, came over to me and burst out, "I don't know what I'm going to do if Sharon dies!"

Gail quickly agreed with her and said, "I can't believe that this hospital doesn't even have a place to pray!" and then more vehemently, "I mean, isn't that what hospitals are all about?" Karen nodded vigorously.

"If there were a place, would you like to pray?" I asked.

They both eagerly agreed and we sat on a bed, holding hands and praying together. Then we discussed their concepts of death. The subject of death had not come up at all during the afternoon or early evening, but in the dark their concerns surfaced and they were ready to talk.

Sometimes children have difficulty expressing their spiritual concerns in words. It is hard enough for adults; children are hindered by their vocabulary or conceptual understanding from articulating their deep experiences. A nurse may be able to help a child express spiritual concerns using symbolic language. Drawing can be a natural and spontaneous expression for a child. Suggest, for example, that he or she draw any of the following: the hospital or clinic, family, diagnosis ("show me what's wrong with you"), something he or she could be (or is) afraid of, what safety or security is like, what God is like or what death is like.[5] Then ask him or her to tell you about the picture, or to tell you a story about it. This can generate helpful communication between child and nurse. One safeguard against misinterpretation (which leads to misdiagnosis) is to summarize the child's interpretation and ask if you have understood the picture.

Liable to Be Labeled

Nursing diagnosis is a fairly new term, but the concept itself is not. It is the product of nursing assessment and can be defined as a "concise summary statement of identified patient problems which are amenable to nursing intervention."[6] The development of nursing diagnosis has been a grassroots movement since 1973, the year of the first national conference of the Clearinghouse for Classification of Nursing Diagnosis. At that time, "Alterations in Faith: in Self, Others and God" was proposed, along with thirty-three other preliminary diagnoses.

After a research project, the second national conference met in 1975 and accepted thirty-seven diagnostic labels, including such diagnoses as confusion, grieving (delayed, anticipatory, acute) and body fluids (depletion and excess). At that time the "alterations of faith" diagnosis was left in the "to be considered" category. Eight regional conferences were held over the next few years to involve more nurses and generate additional background material for the third conference. The San Francisco regional conference had one task force work on the "alterations of faith" category and make a proposal, which was taken to the third national conference in 1978. At that conference the group approved twenty-eight diagnoses, including a revision of "alterations of faith" called "matters of spirituality." The labels accepted under that category were *spiritual concerns, spiritual distress* and *spiritual despair.* Each included a list of defining characteristics and etiologies according to the standardized form required by the clearinghouse.

The final product, reprinted in *The Nurses Lamp* (see Appendix A), appears complex and difficult to use. Although three diagnoses are identified, they are actually a continuum of severity rather than separate patient problems. While the diagnoses are not ideal (they were developed by a committee of about fifteen people who had only parts of three days to come to some agreement) they are useful for two reasons. First, nursing leaders have documented that nurses can and should be involved in spiritual care. Second, they provide a list of defining characteristics (observed signs and symptoms) which provide specific evidences of spiritual need and a framework for intervention.

In order to clarify the spiritual diagnoses accepted by the third national conference, I have correlated their "defining characteristics" with the three spiritual needs described in *Spiritual Care: The Nurse's Role.*[7] To use Table 3 in diagnosis, list all the clues you have gathered about the child or the parents. Categorize them under the following headings: physical, emotional, nonverbal and verbal expressions of a spiritual need (which correspond to the horizontal categories of the chart). Now refer to the chart and see if the clues you have listed appear on the chart. Circle the ones that most closely match what you have observed.

Determine whether the defining characteristics (clues) seem to line up under one spiritual need in particular (that is, one of the three vertical categories). Some clues will point definitely to one specific need; others may provide definite evidence for two or three needs. Remember that the closer a defining characteristic is to the bottom of the chart, the more weight it has in determining a spiritual diagnosis. These verbal expressions zero in most precisely on the spiritual area.

Parents of ill children can experience any of the three spiritual needs; guilt, however, is a common feeling and creates a need for forgiveness. Even parents who, to the objective outsider, had no part in their child's problem may feel somehow responsible. Then there are parents who may have contributed (accidentally or willfully) to their child's problem and are greatly distressed. Both need to know God's forgiveness.

A clergyman told me about a time when he was called to an emergency room. A mother was extremely upset because her son had been severely burned in the bathtub and she was overcome with guilt. After listening to her and talking with her, he offered to pray for her a prayer of absolution. She accepted with obvious relief. After he prayed she became calm and relaxed.

Meeting the spiritual needs of parents is not merely a nice "extra." Parents without resources to deal with their guilt may cause major behavior problems with their chronically or terminally ill children. Parents who have lost hope or who lack trust in God's love and concern cannot adequately support their children.

Step by Step
In looking at the spiritual needs of children, we must consider their developmental levels. I would like to propose that the need for *love and relatedness* is the earliest spiritual need and corres-

Table 3: Spiritual Distress Diagnosis
SPIRITUAL DISTRESS RELATED TO
NEED FOR LOVE AND RELATEDNESS

PHYSICAL/EMOTIONAL DISEQUILIBRIUM		
	Need to establish relationship bewilderment anxiety alienation	*Need to maintain relationship* loneliness sense of abandonment

SPIRITUAL DISEQUILIBRIUM

Non-Verbal Behavior

investigates various beliefs
seeks spiritual assistance
frantically seeks advice or
  support for decisions

attempts to substitute simplified
  rituals in place of usual
  worship
seeks spiritual assistance

Anger toward God {
reluctant to participate in
  spiritual rituals
rebels
displaces anger toward religious
  representative
}

Verbal Expressions

ambivalent about own and
  others' belief systems
verbalizes inner conflict about
  beliefs
questions credibility of religious-
  cultural system
doubts credibility of religious-
  cultural system
sense of spiritual emptiness

expresses concern about
  relation with God/deity
disturbance in concept/percep-
  tion of God or belief system
ambivalent toward God
questions credibility of God/
  belief system
doubts compassion of superior
  being

Remoteness from God {
lacks a feeling of unity with God
feels spiritually empty
gains little satisfaction in prayer
verbalizes that God seems very
  distant
verbalizes desire to feel close
  to God
}

SPIRITUAL DISTRESS RELATED TO NEED FOR FORGIVENESS	SPIRITUAL DISTRESS RELATED TO NEED FOR MEANING AND PURPOSE	
	In life and death	*In suffering*
bitterness	fears (darkness, being alone, going to sleep, etc.)	self-focus (demonstrated by withdrawal, irritability, restlessness, agitation, self-pity, fatigue)
recrimination	feelings of uselessness, hopelessness, meaninglessness	feelings of hopelessness
self-belittling		feelings of powerlessness
projection of blame	demanding behavior	
	apathy, withdrawal	
	cynicism	
	loss of affect	
	depression	
	requires extreme effort to function	
	sense of exhaustion	
inability to forgive self or receive forgiveness	disturbing dreams	self-destructive behavior
self-destructive behavior	avoidance or preoccupation with subject of death	
	discontinued religious participation	
	self-destructive behavior	
	refusal to communicate with loved ones	
wish to undo, redo, relive the past	struggles with meaning in life and death	questions about meaning in suffering
expressions of shame, regret, sinfulness, guilt	questions about meaning of own existence	expression that suffering is necessary reparation
illness seen as punishment from God	concern about life after death	illness seen as punishment from God
doubts about acceptance by God	"gallows" humor	fear of ability to endure suffering
	loss of spiritual belief	
	death wish (escapism)	

Signs of physical/emotional disequilibrium possible in all needs

disturbance in sleep/rest pattern	grief
psychosomatic manifestations	crying
sexual activity disturbance	depression
discouragement	preoccupation
anxiety	anger

ponds with Erik Erikson's stage of trust. The need for *forgiveness* may appear next, paralleling moral development and Erikson's stages of initiative vs. guilt and industry vs. inferiority. I can clearly remember feeling guilty about stealing a bookmark when I was in the fourth grade. God's forgiveness was just as real when I confessed and returned the item. The need for *meaning and purpose* probably develops in early adolescence in normal, healthy children corresponding with the stage of identity vs. role confusion. Children who are hospitalized with serious illness or injuries may be forced to consider the meaning and purpose of their lives at a much earlier age. Many nurses have been amazed at the profound insights expressed by seriously ill youngsters.

The fears that children express also give clues about their spiritual needs. Sally Miller summarizes them as follows:

0-6 mo. sudden movements, loud noises, loss of support, pain

8-12 mo. fear of strangers, strange objects, heights, anticipated situations

2 yrs. noises, strange persons, strange events, falling

2-4 yrs. being alone, darkness, animals (snakes, dogs), imaginary fears (draining bathtubs, vacuum cleaners, ghosts, kidnappers)

4-6 yrs. animals, darkness, bedtime (spooks, ghosts), bad people, physical injury and bodily mutilation

6-12 yrs. punishment, guilt, failure, hell, breaking moral code, natural hazards, disaster, political concerns (war, communist takeover), injury or death of self or loved ones; fear of the supernatural and animals decreasing but still present[8]

Fears become more complex as a child grows older. Many relate to the supernatural and moral realms. Most of these fears can be summarized by the question, "Who, if anyone, is in control?" As children mature they begin to realize that their parents are not omnipotent. Illness and hospitalization intensify this process. Children may wonder why their parents allow medical personnel to perform intrusive and painful procedures on them. Ultimately the question for the child becomes, "Is there a God, and what is he like?'' At this point the process of assessment by the nurse can be instrumental in helping parent and child move closer to asking this crucial question and receiving an answer that is freeing and satisfying.

Chapter Seven
Is God a Teddy Bear? Images of God

Jack L. Rodgers

The creation story tells us that we are made in the image of God. But as I meet children and parents in the crisis of a child's illness, I am left with another impression—we make images of God. Our humanness influences our emotional and spiritual maturation and the nature of our relationship with God. As a hospital chaplain I try to assess what image each parent and child sees.

Catching the Butterfly

At times I feel like a person with a net, trying to catch a butterfly. Just as I feel close to understanding a person's relationship with God, the person changes direction. My own images of God constantly change too as I discover more about God's many-faceted nature. Parents and children who are sick perceive God differently according to their spiritual needs of the moment. Sometimes those perceptions are accurate understandings of the character of God, and sometimes they are attempts to make God in their own images. Job, in his anguish, tried several images of God to understand his tragedy. His comforters added their own images and relationships to Job's, yet left him without comfort.

The way in which a parent relates to God depends on many factors in his or her emotional, moral and spiritual development. Studies suggest that parents tend to relate to their children as they themselves were treated by their parents, unless they have been drastically changed or received insight into their lives. I believe that parents also relate to God during their child's illness as they related (or relate) to their earthly parents. Their children's images and relationships with God will in turn bear the influence of their relationship with the Lord. This cycle can turn vicious, however, because earthly families are not always ideal. They exhibit wide variations of togetherness and distance, love and hate, unity and brokenness, harmony and conflict, maturity and childishness. These variations may influence the parents' and the children's relationships with the heavenly Father too.

I rejoice that God, "our Father who is in heaven," touches his children in earthly ways. Consider the prodigal son, whose primary need was for forgiveness (Lk 15:11-32). The struggle between Joseph and his brothers illustrates human nature at its rawest yet God intervened to redeem the situation (Gen 37—50). Over and over God chose imperfect people with twisted images of him to do his will. Even Jesus' disciples misunderstood his mission until after the resurrection. Is it any wonder that in the midst of crisis parents and children perceive God according to their own hopes, fears and needs?

Certain images are common to parents and children in crisis. I present them in random order and recognize that a person may have more than one image of God at a time. They are also subject to immediate or gradual change. Often they are attempts to make sense out of the nonsense of suffering and sickness. God alone knows the accuracy of each picture, because each of us "can see and understand only a little about God now, as if we were peering at his reflection in a poor mirror" (1 Cor 13:12 TLB).

The Authoritarian Judge

Though the Bible speaks emphatically about God's power, a parent's reaction to a child's illness may overemphasize God's judgment and punishment. "What did I do to deserve this?" they ask themselves; some even feel personally chastised and punished through their child's illness. Many quote Exodus 34:7 that the Lord will punish the children for the sins of their fathers.

Mr. De Antonio sat in the parents' lounge of the intensive care unit, banging his head against the wall. He felt responsible for his son's injury. He had allowed Jeff to play with a hatchet in his workshop. When it fell it cut a deep gash in his son's face. As we spoke he gradually began to reach beyond his self-punishment to see God as punishing him through this accident. His image of God was of an unmerciful, punishing Father who is distant from his sinful son. Jeff recovered well from surgery, but his father's attitude only gradually diminished. He related to Jeff at a controlled distance and with great authority. Soon Jeff's mother took over as his most frequent visitor.

The second day after surgery, Mr. De Antonio requested formal confession with a Catholic priest. Later he described to me his journey to America with his parents. His father was a firm authoritarian who had difficulty expressing love. He spoke warmly of his mother. I struggled to express that our heavenly Father is gracious and merciful, and tried to convey in words and action God's love and care.

The following evening I was called to the chapel to see Mr. Kelly. There he knelt, sobbing uncontrollably. He had just been told that his daughter had cancer. As he gained control, his words and affect expressed his attitude. He believed that he had caused the tragedy because he had made some "shady deals" and had underworld connections. As we prayed, I asked for God's grace through Jesus Christ. Mr. Kelly sought forgiveness and seemed relieved. In the next few days he gained a better understanding of his child's illness. He returned to regular church attendance.

In both cases an earthly influence tainted the father's relationship with God. Both fathers seemed limited to an image of God as authoritarian, which obscured the message of God's forgiveness and love. They could not see the God who chose to suffer with the sufferer. I tried to communicate God's closeness, hoping to replace the image of a distant dealer in punishment.

The String Puller

Sharon is a twenty-year-old kidney transplant patient who recovered well from the procedure. Months later cataracts threatened her with blindness. Through numerous conversations over several months I learned of her strong faith in God. Recently, we talked again. She struggled to decide whether to undergo a risky procedure which might restore her sight. At one point she expressed concern that she might have committed some sin in her past or harbored attitudes which were now clouding her relationship with God. She worried about whether she had hurt God's feelings so that he caused her illness. She finally concluded that God would not be much of a God if this were the crux of their relationship. She would live with the mystery. She decided in favor of the procedure.

Sharon's mother loves her dearly and showed attentive devotion. They seemed to reflect almost identical relationships with God when they tried to make sense out of the transplant complications. The questions I heard from Sharon had been expressed to me by her mother almost verbatim two days before. Both seemed to have guilt feelings without a clear cause. Perhaps each had an upbringing in which discipline was administered through guilt. The sickness was perceived as punishment. They saw God as a "string puller."

The image of a string-puller God is similar to that of the authoritarian judge, but it results from more subtle real or imagined guilt. Parents and older children may react to illness by feeling that they should feel guilty for prior acts or unrecognized sins. Job's comforters encouraged him to look to his past life and present attitude. They assumed him to be guilty, which only increased his pain. Eliphaz said, "Go to God and confess your sins to him" (Job 5:8 TLB).

Job responded, "One should be kind to a fainting friend, but you have accused me without the slightest fear of God. . . . Stop assuming my guilt, for I am righteous" (6:14, 29 TLB). The implication of the comforters was that God allowed Job's tragedy to illicit a confession. My counsel to both Sharon and her mother was to follow Job's refusal of this reasoning. I encouraged them to live with the mystery of asking "Why?"

The Candy Man

Many people view God solely as a gift giver. To them, "God is the candy machine whose purpose is to meet our needs, solve our problems, answer our questions, and give us whatever we happen to want most."[1] During a child's illness what the parent wants most is a miracle: a dissolved tumor, relief from Reyes syndrome, a healthy child. They may expect healing beyond medical possibility. I firmly believe that God does supernaturally intervene to cure; that, however, is not the norm. The frequency of miracles might best be described by one Christian father who said, "God seems to bestow his miracles on believer and nonbeliever without rhyme or reason . . . still I hope." To hope realistically is healthy and helpful, but to hope for complete cure in the face of terminal illness only compounds the distress and alienation of a dying child.

The comforter Bildad seemed to express the candy-man image of God when he said to Job, "If you were pure and good, he would hear your prayer, and answer you, and bless you with a happy home. And though you started with little, you would end with much" (8:6-7 TLB). He believed that God would never say no.

I try to watch for indications that a person has never been denied anything from God or their parents. Often they will expect God to do their bidding. Perhaps ulterior motives are behind their professed faith. Their own parents may have made many promises to God in hopes of gifts in return. I never discourage hope as a real spiritual force which sustains, but always balance realistic hope with prognostic fact. At the same time, I stress the mystery of God's involvement in the child's illness.

Jane, age four, was diagnosed as having a highly malignant bone tumor. Her mother fell to pieces, crying privately and publicly. Her grandmother was also at the hospital, and also very upset. Soon chemotherapy and radiation treatments were begun. The mother had no confessed faith, but soon became a Christian and a member of a charismatic group. Later she joined a local church. She became convinced that Jane would be healed. Jane's clothing was replaced with a new wardrobe, her supply of dolls and stuffed animals doubled, and her mother attempted to satisfy her every need. The grandmother also attempted to satisfy each of her own daughter's requests.

This mother gained hope through her new faith, but it was at the expense of Jane's discipline, realistic hope and normal life. In a few weeks the mother learned to discipline her child with love, giving fewer material gifts and more of herself. She was able to say, "God's will be done" as her relationship with God changed to an assurance that he would see the family through whatever happened.

Jane's condition steadily deteriorated and she eventually died. My benediction prayer centered on "biting our tongue on our own needs while striving toward God's will." I stressed the hope of a heavenly home free from pain, misery and suffering. Jane's mother said, "Amen." She had moved from the "candy man" to the God who sustains us in suffering and accepts our children in love.

The Model
Not all images are negative, however. For example, parents and

children need role models to guide them through the rough waters of illness. They say, "We never had anyone die before" or even ask, "What do we do now?" Biblical characters can serve as examples of how families can relate to God. The dilemma of Job, Jacob's willingness to sacrifice Isaac, Jesus' death on the cross, Paul's thorn in the flesh and the physically infirm in the New Testament can help the parent and child to know that God is with them in their suffering.

Maria had encephalitis as a young child. Later she developed chronic leukemia, with which she suffered the last eight years of her life. I met her three years ago when the disease became severe. We did not talk much about God then, but she openly expressed her anger about the disease and how it limited her active lifestyle. To her death, she fought the disease with courage and outspokenness. Hospital staff said that she "had nine lives."

During one of her last hospital stays she began to talk about her faith. She said that Jesus was her life model. She believed in his love, supported his stands on human justice and applauded his rejection of phony authorities. She knew he was her friend. Only at one point did she stop identifying with him. She was disappointed that Jesus went to the cross so willingly. We struggled with this. She eventually accepted the fact that Jesus had a purpose in dying but her goal was to live. She still had many things to do; Jesus had fulfilled his mission. She enjoyed that difference and continued to fight until the end.

The Teddy Bear

Jesus Christ promised to send us a comforter, the Holy Spirit. Parents and sick children need comfort. They need to feel that God is with them. They fear being abandoned by God while they are suffering. They may feel lonely and afraid to be alone. God's presence and comfort meet real spiritual needs with help and healing.

Eight-year-old John had leukemia. His mother was a deeply committed Christian. His father was also a believer, but his faith was more philosophical than experiential. Several times John's illness went into remission. These were good times which his parents never interpreted as miracles. His mother constantly reminded John and herself of God's presence. She read the Bible and prayed with John daily.

Finally, the leukemia became severe. John would get scared and lash out, but his mother assured him that God understood, cared and was with him—sort of like the bedraggled teddy bear at his side. He could vicariously take the jabs with the syringe and the bops on the head when John was angry, and still be there to comfort him.

Finally, bleeding, mouth ulcers and infection began. John's last admission to the hospital was painful, frightening and long. His mother continued to assure him of God's love, which seemed to comfort him. One day John's mother told me that John was disappointed because he had missed Holy Communion while in the hospital. I offered to bring him the bread and wine if he could tolerate it. John smiled. I returned and conducted a Communion service in his room. Despite the sore ulcers in his mouth he managed to swallow the bread and sip the wine with a straw from a little Communion glass. I reaffirmed God's presence in our closing prayer. John died several days later. That Last Supper was deeply meaningful—to John, to his mother and to me.

John had a special relationship with God. He seemed free to vent his feelings without fear of abandonment by his mother, father or God. God was personal and alive to John in his illness. God was his security—the familiar and unchangeable Being in an unpredictable, painful world. In many ways, God came to John as a teddy bear, willing to take all of his bumps and bruises and anger, and still offer him comfort and forgiveness.

God is not a mere teddy bear. His nature is much fuller, but when people are in need of comfort we are not compelled to round out their theology by presenting God as judge. "After the Lord had finished speaking with Job, he said to Eliphaz the Temanite: 'I am angry with you and with your two friends, for you have not been right in what you have said about me, as my servant Job was' " (Job 42:7 TLB). The truth about God to suffering people is that "the Lord has comforted his people, and will have compassion upon them in their sorrow" (Is 49:13 TLB).

Job's "comforters" failed to comfort because they were more concerned with projecting their image of God onto Job and his problem. They talked more than they listened, increasing his pain. They felt that Job was too comfortable with his image of God. Sometimes when God comes to those who are suffering, he comforts them like a teddy bear. Our job, as comforters, is to help them recognize that comfort.

Chapter Eight
The Suffering of Children
Joseph Bayly

Children suffer, be they infants, youngsters or teens. We often overlook this fact and concentrate on adults; in suffering, as in so many other areas, children are perceived as mere extensions of their parents. Yet they do suffer, and God can work through their suffering. Or Satan can work through it.

It was suffering that led to my calling to the Christian ministry when I was eight years old. My brother, not yet two, required serious surgery, a mastoidectomy. In my bed one night, alone in the dark cold of the mountains of central Pennsylvania, I covenanted with God that if he would make my baby brother well, I would serve him with my life. He did.

On the other hand, suffering can hurt children. A few years ago our daughter told us about a discouraging experience she had when she was nine years old and her four-year-old brother was sick, then died, of leukemia. She said the teachers in a Christian school would scold her when she misbehaved, not realizing that misbehavior is often a sign that a child is suffering: "Haven't your parents suffered enough? Why do you make them suffer more?"

"No one seemed to realize," she now says, "that I was suffering too."

Death Is Not the Only Crisis

Every family experiences crisis: terminal illness and death of a parent or child; chronic illness of a parent or child; birth, growth and planning for a retarded or severely handicapped child; divorce; unemployment and other financial stresses; moving; alcoholism; a depressed or otherwise emotionally ill parent or child; spouse or child abuse; delinquency and crime; or accidents. Dame Cicely Saunders, the British psychiatrist instrumental in founding the hospice movement, says that total pain involves physical, mental, financial, interpersonal and spiritual factors. Children can suffer in any, or all, of these areas.

God works in children through loss and suffering. Who are the most memorable characters in the Bible? Joseph, Daniel, the young girl who served in Naaman's household, Samuel, Isaac— all had traumatic experiences as children. Some were uprooted and taken captive to another country, one was hated and betrayed by brothers, another was almost killed by his father.

Such suffering may produce good effects in children, including patience, courage, the ability to withstand pain, an understanding of their parents and early maturity. Children, however, often struggle to cope with suffering, just as adults do. Who can explain the pain of an infant sister to another child in the family, or the helplessness and strange behavior of a brain-damaged brother? Guilt can compound these struggles. Most children, at some time or another, think or say to a parent or sibling, "I wish you were dead!" If death later occurs, the child may be torn by guilt.

Most parents, including Christians, try to shield their children from suffering. This mistake results from our failure to perceive children as children rather than as little adults. The apostle Paul recognized this: "When I was a child, I spoke like a child, I thought like a child, I reasoned like a child" (1 Cor 13:11). Children can cope, and they grow (as we do) by being forced at times to cope rather than being sheltered.

After our eighteen-year-old son died, we discovered a diary he had kept at the age of eleven, when his five-year-old brother died. Here is an excerpt: "About 1 P.M., something told me to pray for Danny. When I got home from school, I discovered that he had died just then! Debbie and I went up to the bedroom and saw him. We went and looked at a burial ground for four of the family. After we all ate (Daddy arranged for the funeral), a lot of people came over and we read the Bible, sang and prayed."

Two days later his diary entry was this: "Today we had Danny's funeral. There were a lot of flowers. The coffin was white. The service was a blessing. Then we went to see the grave. It was very unhappy, but Danny is with God. After we got home, Jerry Sterrett and I played ball in the yard."

The last sentence indicates an eleven-year-old's point of view. Childhood insulates us from suffering.

The Whole Package

Isolating spiritual needs from other needs of a child or teen at a time of crisis is almost impossible. All needs are intertwined because a child is a unified whole of interrelated and inseparable elements. Effective help in coping with the physical, emotional and interpersonal factors in a crisis may soften or preclude a spiritual need. Failure to help in these other areas may create, intensify or prolong a spiritual need.

A child's problems in coping with crisis or in responding appropriately to loss should only be considered spiritual when we are reasonably sure that other needs have been met. Spiritualizing other needs may easily short-circuit the lengthy and troublesome process of finding complex areas of need which are not spiritual.

Parents are in the best position to provide this help. Unfortunately they often (I am tempted to say usually) do not understand their children's needs or read danger signals. If they do, they are frequently so bruised and beaten themselves that they cannot do much to help their children. They are caught up in their own survival.

Friends, neighbors, the Christian community and teachers could do much to meet these needs of children. Betty Lundberg writes in the *Wesleyan Advocate,* "I have Bell's palsy. One of the positives about my condition is that it lets me be on the receiving end of so many expressions of love. People brought gifts of food and delicious meals night after night. One dear member of our church brought our son's favorite chocolate cake. Karl, my son, sat on the side of my bed eating a large piece and telling me how good it was. When I couldn't do anything for him, I so appreciated others who did."

"You Never Cried"

Children need models of coping with crisis and of grieving in response to loss. Dr. Alice Ginott, child psychiatrist and widow of Dr. Haim Ginott, counseled Israeli war widows. She deplores widows who stoically conceal their grief. Even a two-year-old, she feels, must be told the truth and allowed to mourn the loss of a father, or risk being scarred by emotional damage. Tears can bring together parent and child. This is true not only for a mother; a father should also be a model of grief. Unfortunately in North America men are expected to fulfill a macho image and never cry. Jesus wept. It is recorded twice.

One six-year-old asked his father, "If I died, would you be unhappy?"

The father assured him, "I'd be terribly unhappy. But why do you ask?"

"Because you weren't unhappy when my baby brother died. You never cried."

Children need the assurance that everyone is being honest with them. We may not tell a child everything, but we should tell enough and never lie. A child's fantasies may be worse than the reality (much misinformation may be picked up by a child in a hospital room with other children).

I was asked to counsel a family that had moved to northern Illinois from Florida at Christmastime six years before. The two older boys, six and eight, had gone exploring the day after Christmas. They found a lake. Not knowing that he should test the ice, the older boy ran out on it and fell through. The younger boy ran home screaming for help—and that was the end of it as far as he was concerned. He was not taken to the funeral. He never knew what happened. A taboo was placed on the use of the older child's name. Now, six years later, he is twelve years old and wakes up screaming in the night: he thinks that his brother is still under the ice, that his parents have not done anything. A murderous conflict has arisen between him and his father which might have been prevented by openness and honesty at the time of loss.

Children should never be lied to. When a parent dies we are tempted to say, "Mother has gone away on a trip. She's left us for a time." But Mother will not return and the sooner the child realizes this, the better. I believe that, in most cases, a child should see the body of one who has died, to realize that Mother cannot breathe or talk anymore.

Children take as long as adults to get over a loss. They need time and encouragement to do their grief work. Several years after our losses, Dr. Norvell Peterson, a psychiatrist in New England, suggested that we start conversations about our oldest son who had died: "At dinner, for instance, on relevant occasions such as his birthday or the anniversary of his death, start talking about him. Let the children recall things. Don't sum up or give a sermon." We found this healing for our surviving children . . . and for us.

In his recent book, *Loss, Sadness and Depression,* British psychiatrist John Bowlby says that even children under two years of age respond to loss as adults do. An initial numbness sets in with occasional bouts of intense distress or anger, followed by longing and searching for the lost person. During this period the person is disorganized and in despair. Finally, if grieving accomplishes its purpose, some degree of reorganization begins. The process may take a long time.

Helping Children Cope

The big difference between the losses of children and adults, Dr. Bowlby suggests, is that children are less in control of their circumstances: They are dependent on what adults say and do. Parents must be trained, therefore, to understand their children's needs and be helped to meet them. No one else has the opportunities that parents have to do so. Because of this, organizations such as Compassionate Friends see their responsibility as not merely to help parents recover, but also to help them meet their surviving children's needs.

Sometimes children and teens need special counseling, for instance, when there has been a suicide in the family. The pastor, physician or other advisor should be ready to suggest professional help and to direct them to a specific counselor.

We learned the hard way that spiritual needs must be met. Our son was three years old when his five-year-old brother died of leukemia. My response was to smother him with affection; his mother's was to withdraw from him. Approximately four years later, we were driving to church one Sunday when he said, "I wish I wouldn't think that first thing when I wake up every morning."

"Think what?" I asked.

"I hate God."

Later, when he was ten years old, this same son lost his eighteen-year-old brother. My wife and I did not recognize his needs or know how to meet them. When he became a teen-ager, he rebelled and moved far from Christianity. (We thank God that he has wonderfully returned.)

Parents who lose a child tend to canonize him or her. It is so easy to forget that he needed discipline and punishment or that she was far from perfect. Surviving children observe that image of perfection (which parents usually create unknowingly) and feel that they cannot compete. They may give up.

If a child or adolescent has a congenital problem or a chronic or terminal illness, several considerations are important.

First, the physician should explain the condition carefully and understandably to the parents. It is their right to know the prognosis.

Second, parents often feel guilty and think that God is punishing them through their child's suffering. John 9:1-3 says that this is not necessarily true. In some situations the parents may have contributed to their child's illness by drug use during pregnancy, carelessness or abuse. It is important to emphasize God's forgiveness through Jesus Christ to these parents. Self-blame may easily lead to depression; blaming one another may cut off communication and create distance in a relationship at the very time it is desperately important to parents, to the sick child and to the other children.

Third, parents are, of all people, most vulnerable to those who say, "If you only have faith, God will heal your child of this condition." If you want to help, be sensitive to this and do not promise more than God does.

Fourth, parents pity their suffering children and do special things for them. This reveals how up tight they are. Normal treatment will best communicate their care.

Fifth, concentration on the retarded, handicapped or terminally ill child causes fragmentation of family life. Other children feel neglected—because they are.

God wants to comfort and strengthen suffering children and their families. May we who are close to them be messengers who communicate his care.

Chapter Nine
Ministering to Dying Children & Their Families

Mae Shirley Cook

A father whose fifteen-year-old son had been killed wrote, "Do you know what it is like for me? It's like a gaping cavity right in the middle of my chest, an emotional cavity. No one could live with anything like that physically, and I can barely survive emotionally. That abyss is not being filled—nothing will fill it. In spite of my faith, I have that vapid emptiness."[1] As Christians we believe, we know, that death is not the end of existence, but it is separation. It is the end of a relationship that has special meaning to us in this life.

Death is never beautiful for any living thing: the rose that only yesterday was perfect and velvety, now is wilted; the fledgling bird whose down was soft and feathers were new, now is matted and mud covered; the family dog which a moment before was a bright-eyed, tail-wagging bundle of fur and emotion, now is a stiff, blood-splattered form. The body of a child worn out from a year-long bout with leukemia is not lovely to behold. What thoughts race through a mother's mind as she studies the cold, lifeless body of her little one? Death is the result of sin in our world, and there is no beauty in it.

Death is always a shock to loved ones. No anticipation, no forewarning, no preparation totally cushions the shock. "Shock and unbelief are the first natural reactions to the loss of a loved one. Such is especially true if the person has died suddenly or unexpectedly. But even if there has been a terminal illness, one finds it hard to believe the person is actually gone."[2] The shock is multiplied when a child dies.

What are my feelings about death and dying? What is my attitude as a Christian? Am I able to think about death with a clear, thoughtful mind, or is the very thought repulsive and foreign? Do I cast it out of my mind as quickly as possible?

The Last Enemy

While it is true that Christ has conquered death, as Paul related in 1 Corinthians 15:54-57, it is just as true that we have not. Death is the last enemy to be overcome, as we read in 1 Corinthians 15:26. Do I look forward to the real life that does not begin until this body dies, or is this earthly life the center of my thinking? We can rejoice that those who ran to Jesus' tomb on that first Easter morning did not find the "grim reaper" but an angel.[3]

But can I, do I, face death without fear? How can I relate to a dying child? How can I minister to someone facing death if I am afraid? Do I dare take the time to bare my innermost feelings and thoughtfully consider what the Bible says about death?

Most Christians do not fear death itself, although because it is an unknown dark tunnel it may be very unpleasant to consider. The real fear is, however, of dying. What suffering, ragged emotions, loneliness or financial struggle will be involved? What about loved ones? These thoughts that flood the mind must be dealt with if I am to look at the death of a child in a way that will help others. I must be emotionally involved if I care about a child and his or her family. But I cannot allow myself to be so drained that I am unable to help or share at this strategic time in their lives. Where is the dividing line?

The first step in gaining proper perspective is to acknowledge that God is sovereign in all matters of life and death. This is the starting place if I am to be available and helpful to others. Joseph Bayly in *The View from a Hearse* reminds us, "God is sovereign. That is where we begin to answer questions. Our peace is not in understanding everything that happens, but in knowing He is in control of sickness, health and death itself. We accept life's mysteries and sufferings unexplained because they are known to God —and we know Him."[4]

A Friendship Grows

Matters of life and death are in God's hands but my relationship with a child is in mine. Does Sammy know that I care about him? Does Judy realize that I consider her as much a person as any adult, but with her own needs?

In our hospital Sunday school the teacher returns one afternoon a week to visit those children who were in class the preceding Sunday. There is little time to get acquainted in a busy Sunday-school hour, but relationships grow during those five or ten minutes alone at a bedside or that walk down a hallway pushing a wheelchair. We have time to casually chat about the weather, family, pets and school. It might take weeks to get around to spiritual things. Some relationships do not reach that point before the child leaves the hospital. But if God's love has been communicated to the child in personal conversations, and the way of salvation has been clearly explained in the Sunday-school hour, the rest is in the Lord's hands, especially if there is no means of follow-up.

David came to Sunday school only once, although later I shared a lesson with him in his room. Week after week I stopped by to say hello and leave a small gift. David was so likeable, so mature, so outgoing—and only eight years old. He had leukemia and had already lived longer than his doctors had expected. There never seemed to be time with him alone. Then one day I realized that for three weeks each gift that I had left had on it the very same verse, John 3:16. There had been a pencil with a metal cap, a puzzle and a game (in return, David gave me one of his pencils with his name printed on it). One day his mother remarked that David had felt well enough to print a letter to his sister who was away at camp. She said that David had insisted on copying the Bible verse word for word in that letter. Never underestimate the power of the Word . . . or of friendship!

Evangelism Kid Style
How do you present the way of salvation to a terminally ill child? Simply—as to any child. Most children have no animosity against God. Few join adults in asking, "Why did God let this happen to me?" This is all the more remarkable because in any hospital Sunday school it is possible for a child to be in class one morning . . . and dead the next. Too often the teacher is not aware of how ill a child is. We do, however, carefully explain the way of salvation each week, so simply that each can understand. Every song is chosen to further that message.

One day a mother asked to have all the words of the songs written out, not only for her hospitalized daughter but also for her other two children. She explained that the three children had spent the previous evening singing "Good News" to other children in the room. "In our church they just don't consider the children," she said. "Nothing is on their level. What a help these songs are!"

Each conversation and class lesson must be bathed in prayer. How can anyone know the heart needs of a very sick child after only brief contact? Ah, there is One who does! One who cares more than any person ever could. One who yearns for that child to know him!

Rosalie had visited our Sunday school a few times. As she was helped back to her room she giggled and said, "I hope this doesn't embarrass my rabbi." After she had brain surgery, the Sunday-school aides were told that her mother did not want her in Sunday school anymore because she was not to learn about Jesus. Invariably though, someone would stop by Rosalie's room and invite her to come. Then we would have to explain that she was not allowed to be in class. One morning she cried and yelled, "But I want to go! Who says I can't go?"

We prayed for Rosalie and for her mother. Even as I prayed for the words to say, that mother and I came face to face in the hall outside the girl's room. The mother's first words were, "Who said Rosalie can't go to Sunday school?"

The following Sunday Rosalie was in the front row of the class. The next week she turned to the aide who was pushing her wheelchair back to her room and asked, "Hey, how can I really know I have Jesus in my heart?"

David, the eight-year-old with leukemia, had a special place in our prayers, particularly as he neared the end of his brief life. One warm autumn afternoon I went into his room and found him alone. He needed an oxygen mask, so his words were few. I greeted him and, remembering John 3:16, asked, "David, have you ever asked the Lord Jesus into your life?"

He looked at me over the top of his oxygen mask, a special little guy who was always honest and open. There was no smile, not even a twinkle in his eyes, but his answer was low and clear. "Yes, I did." Then his mother returned to the room and I left, believing the Holy Spirit had done his work.

Just three days later David's mother held him close and whispered, "God wants you, David."

He smiled up at her and said, "Yes, I know!" And he was gone.

The Lord works in as many ways as there are children. After Sunday school Brian told us, "I sat up in my bed and prayed him to come in."

Angela said, "Can I do it right now? Will he come in right this minute?" and being assured that he would, she closed her eyes and prayed.

Johnny said, "I'll do it tonight when I say my prayers. I promise!"

Saying Hi to Jesus

Do you talk to a dying child about heaven? Why not? Most kids of school age and up are aware of how ill they are. Some parents, of course, have taken steps to make sure their children know nothing of their prognoses. But can a child spend time in an oncology ward and not know that leukemia is usually fatal? Each keeps up a pretense that hurts everyone. Family members know they are acting out a lie while the child longs for extra closeness and love.

How beautiful when the opposite is true. Sheryl was only seven years old. She was dying of cancer, and she knew it. She had accepted the Lord as a small child and her constant testimony was of turning to him when the pain became too much for her. She found that his love was always there. She could hardly wait to be with him. Even in their sorrow, her parents could have joy in letting her go, knowing that she understood what was happening and anticipated release from her pain-racked body.

Craig had cancer. With the help of the hospital Sunday-school staff he had accepted the Lord. Only rarely did his family visit, so I made a point of spending time with him. We would talk about Jesus, about heaven and about how wonderful it would be. Jesus was there—and no sickness, no pain. How Craig's face would light up as we talked! One day I said, "Craig, if you get to heaven before I do, will you please say 'hi' to Jesus for me?" He grinned and promised he would.

Sometimes we are not this free to openly share with a child. But we can always pray. Pray that God will open a door for you or for someone else to share his message. Be ready, then, so that the opportunities he gives are not missed. At the close of Sunday school one morning, a nurse requested a Bible. Someone offered a New Testament but she said, "No. It's for Kim's mother. She wants to read to Kim from Ecclesiastes."

Kim's parents were atheists but for some reason wanted to read to her "there's a time to be born and a time to die. . . ." The next day was Kim's time to die. Later, checking through the records, I discovered that on only one morning did Kim's name appear on our list for Sunday school, with a note indicating she wanted someone to come and share the lesson with her in her room. But written above Kim's name was "Didn't see this one." Had she been asleep? Was the doctor with her? Was the curtain drawn around her bed? Why had this opportunity been lost?

An Attitude Check

My personal attitude toward a dying child is vital to my sharing of God's love. I, too, must love, understand and be patient at all times. Each hug, embrace, touch or kiss conveys love.

Eight-year-old Terri had volunteered to sing a solo one morning in Sunday school. The next time we saw her she could not even talk because the spreading cancer and a stroke had incapacitated her. Visits were important because her family seldom came to see her. One day as I stooped to kiss her cheek, Terri's lips moved ever so slightly. It was her kiss in return.

I also prescribe few "don'ts" when dealing with the terminally ill child. First, never pity. To me, kids are the most amazing part of all God's creation. They are unbelievable; they are wonderful! The last thing they want is to be pitied. Second, do not spoil them either. Unacceptable behavior is just as unacceptable in the dying child as in the healthy one. Third, don't say anything you don't mean. Children quickly spot a fake. Spiritual progress can be ruined by a promise that cannot be kept.

My attitude toward a child's condition is also important to my relationship with the Lord. We equate terminal illness and death with old age, not with childhood. Whenever a precious five-year-old or a precocious seven-year-old dies, my relationship with the Lord is tested. I must renew my belief that he never—ever—

makes a mistake (Ps 18:30). I must remember that the Lord did not make the child ill. All illness is a result of Adam and Eve's sin; since their time, illness and death have been part and parcel of the penalty of sin (Gen 3:17-19). I must rest in the fact that he does all things well. His ways are not ours (Is 55:8-9). Furthermore, the Lord is not accountable to me, or anyone, for how he does things.

A healthy attitude should make me alert to the family's attitude. Are they bitter against God? Many are. How often I tried to talk to Anne's grandmother as she faithfully sat beside that dying child. She did not want to hear a word about a God who would allow a child to suffer. Even so, few parents of dying children are atheists. Religious faith can be of tremendous support to a family going through difficult circumstances.

Sometimes that family is seeking answers, perhaps even seeking God himself. Candy's mother always brought her to the hospital Sunday school. Even on Candy's last day on earth, when she was too sick to attend class, her mother kept dropping in on our class, then returning to check on her daughter. She wanted to hear more of the lesson. This opened the door to pray with her and give her a Living New Testament. Today she is a growing Christian, involved in a local Bible study.

Our awareness should also include the fact that a comatose child may still hear and understand. Hearing is usually the last of the senses to be lost. Dana had been to the hospital Sunday school only twice, and had become semicomatose before we learned that her only religious training in all her eleven years had been those brief hours in our classes. Dana's parents were separated and her only sister was also ill, so weeks went by when she had no company. Each time I went to the hospital, I spent some time with Dana. Each time I reminded her of Jesus' love for her, of his death so all could be forgiven for sins, of how wonderful heaven was and, best of all, of the fact that Jesus was there. If Dana believed and loved him, then he was getting ready a very special place just for her. Did she understand? Did she believe? Once as

I sat beside her bed and stroked her hair, telling her how much Jesus and I loved her, she was suddenly restless and struggled. Then her lips formed a single word, "love."

You Can Make a Difference

How can I minister to parents and siblings during this time? First, remember that they are not totally rational because they are under duress. One mother told me of the time she watched her daughter in pain, turned from the bedside, ran out of the house and shook her fist up at the sky. She screamed, "God, I hate you! You can't do this!" Just as quickly she went back into the house, fell on her knees and begged for forgiveness.

Dr. C. Everett Koop has said that if a child is diagnosed as having terminal cancer, the family loses that child twice: once when the diagnosis is made and again at death. Sometimes the second loss is easier to accept.[5]

Second, encourage the family to continue to function as a family. Each has a life to live. When others' needs are forgotten, the tragedy is compounded by a family split. A high percentage of parents with terminally ill or seriously handicapped children are separated or divorced; one estimate is that 90 per cent of these parents develop "serious marital difficulties."[6] This means that in addition to the tragedy of a child's death, a parent is left to cope alone.

Third, foster good communication. Without it, problems will arise. When a family is deeply grieving, members tend to pull away from each other. This happens even in Christian families.

What form can our help take? It is important to suffer with those who suffer. Perhaps nothing communicates the love of the Lord more than to feel their feelings, as best we can. If your tears mingle with a father's as he watches his child gasp for each breath, if you embrace a mother and say, "I love him too" or "My heart aches," then that gesture and those words may narrow any gap.

Whether or not family members are Christians, ask if they would like you to pray with them. Be sensitive to their feelings:

no pressure, no insistence. Sharing a tract, booklet or book might be more appropriate. Many are available that help parents during the traumatic time of anticipating the death of their child. Consider also marking or writing down a verse or passage of Scripture. Be discreet; your purpose is to comfort them, not to meet your evangelism quota.

When possible, be available to meet other needs. Do they need a baby-sitter, a meal or grocery shopping done? Do you have time to spend with the sick child so that other family demands can be met?

Mourn with Those Who Mourn

When a child dies, parents yearn for comfort. The mother longs to be a child again, to climb into her mother's lap and feel comforting arms around her. The father aches to cry like a little boy. Your compassion can be part of the Lord's care for them. Communicate your sympathy, your tenderness, your concern—not by mere words but, more importantly, by your tears and touch. Be a good listener; don't feel that you must talk. Healing can be communicated through these simple means to those whose need for warmth and compassion is so great.

It is not necessarily a time to quote Scripture. It may be more important to visualize with the family what it means to be in the very presence of the Lord. It is a time to assure the family of your prayers, and a time to send a brief letter or a note. In that note share some instance about the child. Notes to parents can open doors to deeper relationships.

A vital area of ministry to a family is after the death of a child. Many do not feel the full impact of death until after the funeral. This is also the time when most folks back off and leave parents and siblings on their own instead of realizing that this is when they most need support. Too many Christians in our day and culture have decided that grief is not for believers. That is so unscriptural: 1 Thessalonians 4:13 does not say not to grieve but not to grieve as those who have no hope. Romans 12:15 tells us to mourn with those who mourn. Grief is God's way of filling the gap, of healing the emotional wound. It is an important time to keep in touch—by phone, by note, by visit.

About a week after the funeral I usually write a letter to those parents with whom I have had any contact. It has been one means of communicating my continuing interest in them, and of sharing my faith in the Lord Jesus Christ. Many letters go unanswered. Imagine my surprise when more than two years after David's death his mother and I were in the same elevator at the hospital. She got off at my floor to talk with me. She said, "You will never know what your letter meant to us after David died! It was so comforting to know that he knew God. I still have that letter. In fact, I think I will go home and read it again!"

Death is amputation. The loss is permanent. The pain will not go away though it will lessen in time. Wounds must heal from the inside out. Loved ones must get the frustration, anger and resentment out of their systems. Don't try to stop them from sharing memories or from talking. It is all part of the healing process and is furthered when you listen.

When you do talk, talk about the child. How terrible if you converse about everyone except that one who is gone. How wrong to pretend the child never existed. Some take this approach out of fear of re-opening the awful wound; again, that wound can only heal from the inside.

If a child really meant something to you, ask for his or her photograph. The response may amaze you! Some parents will thank you again and again and doors will be opened for you to share God's love. Betty was young, unmarried . . . and the mother of two girls. Linda, her younger daughter, died at age seven during open-heart surgery. Betty is somewhat slow of thought, as well as socially and economically disadvantaged. But a visit and supper at a fast-food restaurant did amazing things. She had the opportunity to talk (and talk and talk) about her Linda. Without being asked, she offered photos of her daughter. Jenny, her ten-year-old, willingly accepted a Bible and renewed her interest in a Bible correspondence course. Both girls had written to me that they had accepted the Lord through these courses. Betty accepted some devotional materials and said that she wanted to "get back close to the Lord." As a child she had made a commitment to him but had wandered away. A year later Betty was very involved in a Bible correspondence course herself and had turned down a "live-in" situation, saying, "I want to live for Jesus."

Sympathy is so necessary. Remember, though, that unless you have lost a child, you cannot completely understand the feelings of a bereaved parent. Perhaps, however, you know a parent who can. I knew a young mother whose daughter had died. She was not only unwed but also came from a totally unsupportive family. I knew another mother, a dear Christian whose son had recently died. That home also lacked a father. I wrote to the second mother, sharing the situation of the needy young woman. By return mail came a note which said, "Please do me a big favor and send me her address. We have so much in common."

The Other Children

After years of watching television nothing much will shock children. The problem is that TV is a world of make-believe. Children have so much to learn about living, about values and about the quality of life. What is the impact of all the death and dying on TV? Do kids believe it is not for keeps when the actor who was killed this week shows up next week in another series? Dr. Roberta Temes, psychiatrist and bereavement counselor, says, "Today's parents discuss subjects like sex with their children at an earlier age than ever, but most parents avoid the subject of death. They do so because they themselves are uncomfortable with the subject, so they pretend that they are going to live forever. Yet death is an inevitability. You might say life is a terminal disease."[7]

Janie had terminal cancer and had lost her hair because of chemotherapy. She was still able to go to school and wore a hat every day. Often the other kids teased her. Then her wise mother talked with her teacher and they decided on a course of action.

The teacher spent the weekend researching cancer. That Monday Janie went to school without her hat. The teacher called her to the front of the room and together they explained to the class all they knew about cancer. (Janie, age ten, had asked the doctor many questions and knew much about the disease.) From that day until Janie could no longer go to school, the kids treated her with respect. They had learned about cancer and, more importantly, they had learned about life.

The siblings of a child who has died can know sorrow and loss. They can cope and show amazing understanding. But they, too, need help. A child who is ill rightly gets much attention, but what happens to brother or sister during those long months? How especially difficult it is if only one other child is at home, left to feel unloved or unwanted as all energies are directed to the one who is sick. Can you befriend such children? Take them on an outing? Invite them over for a meal, for an evening, or an hour of TV? Make them feel wanted, loved and important, perhaps let them talk out their own problems and frustrations. Your compassion and appropriate sharing of Jesus' love can help them with their struggles.

"As soon as a child is old enough to love something that can be lost, he is a candidate to becoming a man of sorrows and acquainted with grief."[8] How much they need our help and understanding through difficult days and weeks that surround the death of a brother or sister. Here again is an opportunity to show that you love them by continuing your contact with them—a picnic, a baseball game, a small gift when you visit their home. They who have lost a much-loved brother or sister may now gain a much-needed friend.

All the pathos, trauma and heartache of this mixed-up, sin-laden world seem to combine in the terminal illness and death of a child. What more appropriate time is there for each of us to share God's unending, ever-reaching love?

Chapter Ten
Dealing with Feelings of Inadequacy
Susan K. Reed

Meeting the spiritual needs of children and their families sounds like a good idea. I know that I should do it, but I feel inadequate! I am in my second year out of nursing school, with all the rights, privileges, frustrations and tears that come with the status. I work in a children's hospital as a staff nurse in the pediatric intensive care unit (PICU). Last year I worked on a general medical-surgical floor. You know the one: intravenous pole races, wheelchair relays, hard rock blaring from the teen room, trying to find kids when it's time for their medications, then trying to convince them that they really do want to take them.

In the PICU I can be more organized, concentrating my attention on one or two children rather than twenty-two. Both the floor and the PICU have their stresses and challenges in different ways. Somehow all the books and articles I studied in school compound my feelings of inadequacy, because I am not able to do all those neat things which are so important. The authors made it sound effortless, but I struggle. Often I go home feeling like an inexperienced failure. Over and over I have to remind myself that I am giving safe and adequate care, and that the Lord is helping me grow, even through my mistakes.

These Very Special People

Kids are the greatest. I consider it a real privilege to work with them. Jesus treasured them and told his disciples, "Let the children come to me, do not hinder them; for to such belongs the kingdom of God" (Mk 10:14). He told people to become like children in their humility, trust, dependency and love.

I enjoy the inquisitiveness of children and their eagerness to participate in their care. I remember one nine-year-old boy with cystic fibrosis who was being hospitalized for the first time since infancy. He was determined to learn the lingo, procedures and everything else pertaining to the hospital routine. He memorized his medication schedule and would appear at my medicine cart at precisely the right time with his IV pole in hand, the correct amount of fluid in his Buretrol, everything ready for his hook-up to the heparin well.

At first I was unsure whether I could tolerate working with sick children, but now I cannot imagine working with anyone other than these very special people. But that doesn't make it easy. I must constantly remind myself of why I love working with kids in order to meet the challenges that arise. Among the challenges are the spiritual needs of the kids in my care. Identifying these needs is the half of the battle in which I feel fairly confident. Meeting the needs is much more difficult.

Cathy had cystic fibrosis but, because her disease had been relatively mild, she had avoided hospitalizations for most of her nineteen years. When she was finally admitted to the hospital, she seemed deeply concerned as she met other teens in more advanced stages of the disease and learned how they coped. Cathy maintained a cheerful appearance, with her friendly manner and wild jokes, but inside she battled an overwhelming depression.

As I was checking her IV one day, I noticed that her eyes were red and teary. I sat down beside her bed and gently asked her what was wrong. She poured out her frustrations. "How can I get a job, or be independent, when I'm always getting sick? Someone will always have to take care of me." Through a stream of tears she told me about some of her job experiences and her poor relationship with a landlady. Then she began talking about John, a twenty-one-year-old with cystic fibrosis, who was staying in the next room. "You know, John is such a neat guy. He seems to have his head together better than I do. I don't know—there's something different about him."

"Well," I said, "maybe it has something to do with his faith. He told me that he knows Christ will not let him down, even when things seem to be going all wrong."

"Yes, he was telling me about that too. That's really great for him, but I don't think it would work for me. . . ."

Our conversation was cut off by various interruptions and calls to the front desk. I never got another chance to talk with Cathy alone. I feel that I did not help her much. I listened; that may have helped her feel better. I tried to start another conversation about Jesus Christ, but that was interrupted and never completed. I wonder if perhaps I cut off Cathy's expression of her own needs by picking up on John and holding him up as a model. Maybe Cathy wasn't ready for that.

Am I Weird?
Meeting spiritual needs is a priority that I do not want to push aside. I want Christ to shine through me in all that I do, but too often my own needs, frustrations and lack of experience get in the way. I also have a natural desire, working in a secular setting, to be liked;

sometimes I find myself holding back when I want to talk about my faith, for fear of being considered weird.

Four main resources and sources of support help me in my struggle. God continually reveals himself as I spend time in the Scriptures each day. Jesus' experiences show that he is deeply compassionate and sensitive to my day-to-day struggles (Heb 4:15-16). Another source of strength is prayer. "God is our refuge and strength, a very present help in trouble" (Ps 46:1). The times I have spent praying with others and the times when others were praying for me have greatly influenced me and helped me grow. I am excited to see how God continually answers prayer.

Nurses Christian Fellowship provides many opportunities for meeting and sharing with Christian nurses. A more experienced Christian nurse and I have studied the Bible together, using NCF materials designed to apply Scripture to everyday situations in nursing. NCF also has small group Bible studies for nurses and nursing students, special workshops where Christian nurses can learn from one another and a wide selection of publications.

Finally, the support I receive from my Christian brothers and sisters strengthens me to meet the challenges in all areas of my life. Compassion, anger, grief and a myriad of other emotions seem overwhelming at times. Having someone to listen to me and give me feedback helps me to better understand what I am feeling and how I can deal with it. Even in the secular setting of the hospital, I have been amazed at how God has led me to other staff members who are Christians and to Christian families of children in the hospital.

Yvonne, age thirteen, was admitted to the PICU with Reyes syndrome, stage II, a diagnosis that made us shudder. Two of us took care of her that first night, making sure all procedures and supportive therapy were carried out. We protected her as she thrashed about, totally unaware of her surroundings. My heart ached for her parents as they came in periodically to see their daughter. During the night, when things were calm, I sat by her bed and asked the Lord to heal Yvonne. The next morning,

Trudy, another Christian nurse in the unit, told me that Yvonne's parents were Christians. That night Yvonne's condition deteriorated; our prayers became more fervent.

"Trudy," the evening nurse said in report, "Yvonne's parents wanted to know if you'd be here. Something about you knowing the same Christ as they do. That's cool, I guess."

When we came in the next night Yvonne had improved. She was disconnected from the respirator, ICP monitor and arterial line. She was alert and knew where she was. During report one nurse commented, "I wonder what we did differently in this case." Trudy and I glanced at each other, sharing a moment of joy and praise. Early the next morning I met Yvonne's parents in the hall and shared their joy. What an encouragement this experience had been to my faith!

Many situations at work are terribly painful and cause me to ask, "Why?" I think particularly of the abused children I have cared for in the PICU. One time my anger soared when the drunken father of a severely abused child threatened me because he did not feel I was caring for his child properly. The situation was beyond my understanding. God, however, is sovereign. Though we do not understand many things now, someday they will be clearly revealed to us. In the meantime, we can affirm that God is in control and can be trusted.

I doubt whether I will ever completely overcome my feelings of inadequacy, especially when I look at my track record, but I know that God is adequate. Every new experience I encounter brings the opportunity for challenge and new growth. I have found it important to listen and learn from children, their parents, experienced nurses and other child-care workers.

I would like to revive some of the dreams I had back in nursing school, and add to them new dreams of better care for the whole child and the whole family as I gain more experience and put my beliefs into practice. In the meantime, I find it most important to remember my greatest resource of all—my best friend and Lord, Jesus Christ.

Appendix A
The Patient's Spiritual Needs—
A Part of Nursing Diagnosis

Matters of Spirituality

Definition:

Spirituality—the life principle that pervades a person's entire being, his volitional, emotional, moral-ethical, intellectual and physical dimensions, and generates a capacity for transcendent values.

The spiritual dimension of a person integrates and transcends the biological and psychosocial nature.

References:

Sr. Martha Liening. "Spiritual Needs of the Psychiatric Patient" in Lois Dunlap (ed.) *Mental Health Concepts and Nursing Practice*. New York: Wiley, 1978, Chapter 7.

"The term 'spiritual' is often used interchangeably or synonymously with 'religious,' but the terms are not the same. If they are used synonymously or interchangeably as a basis for assessment of nursing needs, some of the patient's deepest needs may be glossed over or entirely overlooked. Spiritual care implies a much broader grasp of that search for meaning that goes on within every human life and which emerges so much more insistently in the life of the person who is mentally ill.

"The White House Conference on Aging refers to spiritual needs as the 'deepest requirement of the self which, if met, makes it possible for the person to function with a meaningful identity and purpose so that in all stages of life the person may relate to reality with hope.'[1] In its simplest concept the word 'spirit' is often equated with the 'breath of life,' the animating principle of the physical organism. The term 'spiritual' may at times be rather vaguely understood, but it can be said to encompass those needs which stem from the thinking, feeling, motivating forces which influence us in our search for meaning and for our inner strivings toward those goals in life which hold the deepest values for us."

Peipgras, Ruth. "The Other Dimension: Spiritual Help," *Americal Journal of Nursing*, 68:12:2610 (December 1968).

" . . . spiritual help is different from emotional support. Whereas the latter concerns itself with the relationship of a person to himself and his environment, the former concerns a person's relationship to a higher being. . . . Spiritual longing is often made manifest by the emotions. . . . Although spiritual and emotional struggles may be intertwined, emotional support alone does not approach the root of his problem; it will not help the person whose need is spiritual."

I. Spiritual Concerns
Etiology
Challenged belief system
Separation from religious cultural ties
Anticipated role change
Concerned about relationship with God
Unresolved feelings about the concept of death
Search for more meaning or purpose in existence
Disrupted religious practices

Defining Characteristics
Investigates various beliefs
Verbalizes inner conflict about beliefs
Questions credibility of religious cultural system
Discouraged
Mild anxiety
Bewildered
Anticipatory grief
Questions meaning for own existence
Concern about relationship with God/deity
Unable to participate in usual religious practices, i.e., daily prayers, Communion, meditation, worship services
Attempts to substitute simplified rituals in place of usual worship
Unable to obtain specific foods required by faith/belief system

II. Spiritual Distress
Etiology
Separation from religious cultural ties
Challenged belief and value system
Sense of meaninglessness/purposelessness
Remoteness from God
Disrupted spiritual trust
Moral-ethical nature of therapy
Sense of guilt/shame
Intense suffering
Unresolved feelings about death
Anger toward God

Defining Characteristics
Common to All Etiologies
(One of the following must be present)
Struggling with meaning in life/death
Seeks spiritual assistance
Disturbance in concepts/perception of God or belief system
Disturbance in sleep/rest pattern
Moderate to severe anxiety
Crying
Varying degrees of grieving
Depression
Preoccupation
Psychosomatic manifestations
Degrees of anger
Degrees of guilt

Defining Characteristics
Related to the Above
Specific Etiologies
Separation from Religious Cultural Ties
    Loneliness
    Sense of powerlessness
    Doubts credibility of religious cultural system
Challenged Belief and Value System
    Ambivalent about own and others' belief systems
    Difficulty in receiving assistance
Sense of Meaninglessness/Purposelessness
    Cynicism
    Considers suicide
    Questions meaning in suffering
    Feelings of uselessness
    Withdrawal
    Apathy

Self-destructive behavior
Sexual activity disturbance
Remoteness from God
  Lacks a feeling of unity with God
  Sense of spiritual emptiness
  Gains little satisfaction in prayer
  Verbalizes that God seems very
    distant
  Verbalizes a desire to feel close
    to God
Disrupted Spiritual Trust
  Doubts compassion of superior
    being
  Worries about loss of trust
  Ambivalence
  Resentment
  Feelings of alienation
Moral-Ethical Nature of Therapy
  Sense of powerlessness (trapped
    feeling)
  Ambivalence in decisions
  Questions or refuses therapeutic
    regime
  Agrees to morally/ethically
    unacceptable therapy
  Frantic seeking of advice or support
    for decision making
Sense of Guilt/Shame
  Wish to undo, redo, relive the past
  Expression of shame, regret,
    sinfulness, guilt
  Bitterness, recrimination
  Inability to forgive self or receive
    forgiveness
  Views illness as punishment from
    God
  Doubts acceptance by God
  Self-belittling
  Projection of blame
  Self-destructive behavior
  Sexual activity disturbance

Intense Suffering
  Questions meaning of suffering
  Fear of ability to endure suffering
  Ambivalence toward God
  Questions credibility of God/belief
    system
  Expresses that suffering is
    necessary reparation
  Self-focus as demonstrated by
    withdrawal, irritability,
    restlessness, agitation, self-pity
    or fatigue
Unresolved Feelings about Death
  Fears (i.e., darkness, being alone,
    going to sleep, etc.)
  Concern about life after death
  Disturbing dreams
  "Gallows" humor
  Demanding behavior
  Avoidance/preoccupation with
    subject of death
Anger toward God
  Feels resentment, hostility,
  alienation
  Perceives illness as punishment
    from God
  Reluctance to participate in spiritual
    rituals
  Rebelliousness
  Displacement of anger toward
    religious representative
III. Spiritual Despair
Etiology
Self-disintegration
Lack of will to live
Lost belief in self
Lost belief in treatment
Lost belief in value system and/or God
Defining Characteristics
Hopelessness
Sense of meaninglessness

Loss of spiritual belief
Death wish (escapism)
Sense of exhaustion
Sense of abandonment
Sees no meaning in suffering
Requires extreme effort to function
Withdrawal
Severe depression
Loss of affect
Refusal to communicate with loved
   ones
Discontinued religious participation

**Etiologies for Future
Consideration with Defining
Characteristics**

Religious Immaturity

Unclear differentiation regarding
   beliefs/values ("I believe what I
   was taught")
Feels no freedom of religious choice
Persistent indecision about spiritual
   beliefs
Motivated by self-gratification
Verbalizes little about religious
   meaning in relation to health/illness
Excessive verbalization about spiritual
   relation to health/illness
No verbalization of feelings, acts and
   experiences related to belief system
Lack of integration; behavior
   incongruent with stated belief
Evidence of magical thinking
Uses religious themes to manipulate
   people
Dabbling in a variety of religious
   experiences
Inability to make commitment, closed
   to growth

**Distorted View of Basic
Religious Tenets**

Guilt

Sees illness as punishment
Inadequate substitution of rituals

**Unresolved Hostility toward a
Particular Church, Religion,
Religious Representative**

Anger
Cynicism
Outburst
Refusal to accept visitation by religious
   representative

Group members who prepared the documents
on "Matters of Spirituality" were:
   Claire Campbell, Dallas, TX
   Barbara Fisher, Toronto, Ontario
   Becky Fleeger, Manhattan Beach, CA
   Anne Kuempel, Austin, TX
   Trudi McFarland, Oakton, VA
   Eileen Otis, New Orleans, LA
   Luella Penner, Hudson, WI
   Marie Prince, Sault Ste. Marie, Ontario
   Arlene Thompson, London, Ontario
   Sr. Joyce Turnbull, San Francisco, CA
   Judy Van Heukelem, San Bruno, CA
   Eleanor Vogel, St. Paul, MN
   Group facilitators were:
   Maria Meyer, St. Louis, MO
   Pat Stelzer, St. Louis, MO

Place: St. Louis, Missouri
Date: April 1978
Event: The Third Nursing Conference on
Classification of Nursing Diagnosis

Reprinted from *The Nurses Lamp* 30, No. 1,
September 1978.

[1]"Spiritual Well-Being," White House Conference on Aging, 1971, p. 1.

Appendix B
Nurses Christian Fellowship

Crisis exists on every hand—birth, death, separation, marriage, accident, war, failure. Nurses and nursing students face these and are continually confronted with those who experience them. In crises, people are often more aware of their need for God and for caring people. Nurses Christian Fellowship (NCF) seeks to better prepare nurses and professionals to assist people spiritually, psychosocially and physically as they face crisis. The concern of NCF is for quality nursing care which includes the spiritual dimension and reflects Jesus Christ.

Nurses Christian Fellowship began in Chicago in the mid 1930s with a handful of nurses who shared this concern. In 1948 it was organized nationally with three purposes: (1) to point men and women in nursing who are searching for meaning and purpose in life to Jesus Christ who said, "I am the way, and the truth, and the life"; (2) to urge nurses and students in graduate and undergraduate programs to meet for Bible study, prayer and fellowship that they might become more mature spiritually and increasingly reflect Christlike attitudes and behaviors both personally and professionally; and (3) to declare God's concern for worldwide evangelization and encourage nurses to have a vital role in it.

Toward these ends NCF offers a number of resources. *The Nurse's Role in Spiritual Care Workshops* are designed for graduates and upper-level students. *Love That Heals Seminars* train nurses and nonprofessionals. Summer conferences give students and nurses exposure to God's Word and the spiritual dimension of nursing.

Nurses Christian Fellowship also serves over 150 autonomous student groups across the country which espouse NCF's purposes. Together with faculty, nurses and the assistance of more than 30 NCF staff, these groups aim to integrate their faith with their nursing practice.

Literature provided by NCF is another important resource for these individuals and groups. *The Nurses Lamp,* a bimonthly publication, the Missionary Nurse Survey and Bible study guides are all available through the address below.

Officially Nurses Christian Fellowship is a department of Inter-Varsity Christian Fellowship (IVCF) which is incorporated in the state of Illinois as a nonprofit religious corporation. NCF is represented on IVCF's Board and Corporation by nurses active in the profession. They, together with NCF staff, assist the director and area directors in formulating the program. NCF is represented regularly at the ANA, NLN, NSNA and various state nurses conventions with an exhibit. With no guaranteed income, NCF is dependent on the gifts and prayers of Christian men and women to meet its budget.

Those desiring more information about NCF may write to Nurses Christian Fellowship, 233 Langdon Street, Madison, Wisconsin 53703.

Notes

Chapter 1
[1]Wayne E. Oates, *The Psychology of Religion* (Waco, Tex.: Word, 1973), p. 88.
[2]Barbara L. Nichols, "Special Commission on the Unmet Health Needs of Children and Youth" (Kansas City: American Nurses Association, 1979).
[3]Oates, p. 89.
[4]Sharon Fish and Judith Allen Shelly, *Spiritual Care: The Nurse's Role* (Downers Grove, Ill.: InterVarsity Press, 1978), p. 39.
[5]Erik H. Erikson, *Childhood and Society,* 2nd ed. (New York: W. W. Norton & Co., 1963), pp. 249-50.
[6]Arthur T. Jersild, *The Psychology of Adolescence,* 2nd ed. (New York: Macmillan Co., 1963), pp. 376, 381.

Part I: Introduction
[1]Merton P. Strommen, ed., *Research on Religious Development* (New York: Hawthorn Books, 1971), p. 110.
[2]Robert J. Havighurst and Barry Keating, "The Religion of Youth," *Research on Religious Development,* p. 688.

[3]Ibid., pp. 485-520.

Chapter 2
[1]See Luke 1:44 for an example of a child responding to God while still in the womb.
[2]Erikson, pp. 247-63.
[3]Ibid., pp. 250-51.
[4]Paul D. Meier, *Christian Child Rearing and Personality Development* (Grand Rapids, Mich.: Baker Book House, 1977), p. 91.
[5]Erikson, pp. 249-50.
[6]Based on a 1980 study conducted at Cedars-Sinai Medical Center, Los Angeles, by Donna Stewart, Assistant Director of Nursing.
[7]Erikson, pp. 251-54.
[8]Ibid., pp. 255-58.
[9]Meier, pp. 29-31.
[10]Marilyne B. Gustafson, "Puppets in the Nursing Process," *Supervisor Nurse,* November 1980, pp. 33-35; Karen Ann McLeavey, "Children's Art As an Assessment Tool," *Pediatric Nursing,* March/April 1979, pp. 9-14.
[11]Philip Barker, *Basic Child Psychiatry,* 2nd ed. (Baltimore: University Park Press, 1976), p. 10.
[12]Dorothy R. Marlow, *Textbook of Pediatric Nursing,* 5th ed. (Philadelphia: W. B. Sauders Co., 1977), p. 613.

Chapter 3
[1]Erikson, pp. 255-58.
[2]Marlow, p. 720.
[3]Ronald Goldman, *Readiness for Religion* (London: Routledge and Kegan Paul, 1965), p. 8.
[4]A. Roger Gobbel, "Teaching the Bible with Children: Not How Much, But How?" *Learning With,* January 1981, pp. 1-2.
[5]Goldman, p. 106.
[6]Ibid., p. 103.
[7]Ronald Duska and Mariellen Whelan, *Moral Development: A Guide to Piaget and Kohlberg* (New York: Paulist Press, 1975), pp. 17-18.
[8]David Fassler, "The Young Child in the Hospital," *Young Children* (Journal of the National Association for the Education of Young Children), September 1980, p. 20.
[9]Duska and Whelan, pp. 28-29.
[10]Ibid., p. 46.
[11]Goldman, p. 105.

Chapter 4
[1]Merton P. Strommen et al., *A Study of Generations* (Minneapolis: Augsburg, 1972), p. 229.
[2]Havighurst and Keating, pp. 714-15.
[3]For the initial study, the survey was taken in a Christian high school in California (180 students), a Youth for Christ group in Wisconsin (56 youths) and a Lutheran Church in America congregation in Pennsylvania (27 youths). Results were similar in each sampling. The same questionnaire was used later with eight patients in a children's hospital in Philadelphia with very similar results.
[4]Arthur T. Jersild, Judith S. Brook and David W. Brook, *The Psychology of Adolescence* (New York: Macmillan Co., 1978), p. 549.

[5]Strommen et al., pp. 239-58.
[6]The Gallup Opinion Index, *Religion in America,* 1977-78, pp. 3-4.
[7]"National Institute on Drug Abuse Report" *Reader's Digest,* July 1981, p. 17.
[8]Havighurst and Keating, p. 715.
[9]Ibid.
[10]Susie M. Setzer, "The Adolescent Thinker," *Learning With,* February 1981, p. 3.
[11]Havighurst and Keating, p. 688.
[12]Ibid., p. 715.
[13]Setzer, p. 5.
[14]David P. Ausubel, Raymond Montemayor and Pergrouhi Svajian, *Theory and Problems of Adolescent Development,* 2nd ed. (New York: Grune and Stratton, 1977), p. 245.
[15]André Godin, "Some Developmental Tasks in Christian Education," *Research on Religious Development,* pp. 118-49.
[16]Ausubel, Montemayor and Svajian, p. 247.
[17]Godin, p. 134.
[18]Ibid., p. 149.
[19]Martin L. Hoffman, "Development of Internal Moral Standards in Children," *Research on Religious Development,* pp. 211-54.
[20]Havighurst and Keating, p. 710.
[21]Ibid.
[22]Godin, p. 143.
[23]Erikson, pp. 261-63.

Chapter 6

[1]For further information see "The Religion of Maturity," chapter three in *The Individual and His Religion* by Gordon W. Allport (New York: Macmillan Co., 1950).
[2]Mary Jo Aspinall, "Nursing Diagnosis—The Weak Link," *American Journal of Nursing,* July 1976, pp. 433-37.
[3]Questions were developed by a task force at the Spiritual Needs of Children Workshop, October 19-20, 1979; sponsored by Nurses Christian Fellowship and held at Children's Hospital of Philadelphia.
[4]June Kicuchi, "How the Leukemic Child Chooses His Confidant," *Canadian Nurse,* May 1975, pp. 22-23.
[5]McLeavey.
[6]Andrea Bircher, "On the Development and Classification of Diagnosis," *Nursing Forum* 14 (1975):10-29.
[7]Fish and Shelly, pp. 35-53.
[8]Sally R. Miller, "Children's Fears: A Review of the Literature with Implications for Nursing Research and Practice," *Nursing Research,* July/August 1979, pp. 217-21.

Chapter 7

[1]Shirley C. Guthrie, Jr., "The Narcissism of American Piety," *The Journal of Pastoral Care* 31 (1977).

Chapter 9

[1]H. S. Vigeveno, *Dear David* (Glendale, Calif.: Regal, 1977), p. 10.
[2]D. P. Brooks, *Dealing with Death: A Christian Perspective* (Nashville: Broadman Press, 1974), p. 51.
[3]Vigeveno, p. 66.
[4]Joseph Bayly, *The View from a Hearse* (Elgin, Ill.: David C. Cook, 1969), p. 104. In 1973

a revised edition was published, *The Last Thing We Talk About.*

[5]C. Everett Koop, "What I Tell the Parents of a Dying Child," *Moody Monthly,* October 1976.

[6]Harriet Sarnoff Schiff, *The Bereaved Parent* (New York: Crown Publishers, 1977), p. 57.

[7]Barbara Varro, "Helping Children Cope with Death," *Philadelphia Evening Bulletin,* February 21, 1978.

[8]John Claypool, *Tracks of a Fellow Struggler* (New York: Pyramid, 1974), p. 86.

Contributors

Joseph Bayly is vice president of David C. Cook Publishing Company and general director of the Christian Medical Society. He is a frequent speaker at seminars on death and dying, and the author of several books including *The Last Thing We Talk About, Heaven* and *Winterflight.* He and his wife, Mary Lou, are the parents of six children, three of whom died in childhood.

Mae Shirley Cook, a graduate of Philadelphia College of the Bible, is coordinator of hospital ministries for Handi*Vangelism, a division of the Bible Club Movement. She lives in Philadelphia.

Lois J. Hopkins has an M.S. in nursing education and is an associate professor of nursing at Kent State University in Kent, Ohio.

June Lynn Jones is an assistant professor of nursing at Northern Kentucky University. Formerly on the nursing faculty of Biola College, she has an M.S.

Susan K. Reed, a staff nurse at the Children's Hospital of the King's Daughters in Norfolk, Virginia, received her B.S.N. from Eastern Mennonite College. She spends her summers as a camp nurse in the Norfolk area.

Jack L. Rodgers is a graduate of Alderson-Broaddus College and Eastern Baptist Seminary. He worked as an orderly while attending college, spent nine years as a pastor, and has extensive training both as a chaplain and in supervision for clinical pastoral education. He is currently the chaplain at Children's Hospital of Philadelphia.

Judith Allen Shelly, associate director of resource development for Nurses Christian Fellowship, received her B.S.N. from the Medical College of Virginia and an M.A.R. from Lutheran Theological Seminary at Philadelphia. She is coauthor (with Sharon Fish) of *Spiritual Care: The Nurse's Role,* and author of *Spiritual Care Workbook, Caring in Crisis* and *Dilemma: A Nurse's Guide for Making Ethical Decisions.* She and her husband live in Pennsylvania.

Janet V. Snyder has an M.Ed. and is a nursery-school teacher in Philadelphia.

Susan F. Stanhope is a pediatric staff nurse in Patterson, New York. She has a B.S.N.

Dianne Stannard received her B.S.N. from the University of Wisconsin at Madison. Since graduation she has been a staff nurse and assistant head nurse at Atlanta's Egleston Hospital for Children.

Donna D. Stewart is a registered nurse and serves as assistant director of nursing at Cedars-Sinai Medical Center in Los Angeles.

Marcia Thompson received an M.A.R. and served as director of Christian education in Philadelphia. She now holds that post as a missionary to a church in West Berlin.

Judith Van Heukelem received her B.S.N. from the University of Colorado and M.S. in maternal-child health nursing from the University of California at San Francisco. She has worked in a pediatric intensive care unit and was head nurse in a pediatric research unit. She lives in California and is West regional director of Nurses Christian Fellowship.

Melanie Van Sant has an M.S.N. and is instructor of maternal-child health at the University of Delaware.